WHY NOT EVERY MAN?

*African Americans and Civil Disobedience
in the Quest for the Dream*

George Hendrick

Willene Hendrick

Ivan R. Dee
CHICAGO

www.ivanrdee.com

Library of Congress Cataloging-in-Publication Data:
Hendrick, George.
    Why not every man? : African Americans and civil disobedience in the quest for the dream / George Hendrick, Willene Hendrick.
        p. cm.
    Includes bibliographical references (p.   ) and index.
    ISBN 1-56663-609-4 (cloth : alk. paper) — ISBN 1-56663-645-0 (paper : alk. paper)
    1. African Americans—Civil rights—History. 2. Civil disobedience—United States—History. 3. Civil rights movements—United States—History. 4. Slavery—United States—History. 5. United States—Race relations. 6. Thoreau, Henry David, 1817–1862—Political and social views. 7. Gandhi, Mahatma, 1869–1948—Political and social views. 8. King, Martin Luther, Jr., 1929–1968—Political and social views. I. Hendrick, Willene, 1928– II. Title.
    E185.H49 2005
    303.6′1′08996073—dc22

                                2004062835

For Sarah and Eric, Emilie and Dennis

CONTENTS

WHY NOT EVERY MAN?

INTRODUCTION:

WHY NOT EVERY MAN?

Didn't my Lord deliver Daniel, deliver Daniel, deliver Daniel,
Didn't my Lord deliver Daniel,
An' why not every man?

He delivered Daniel from de lion's den,
Jonah from de belly of de whale,
An' de Hebrew chillun from de fiery furnace,
An' why not every man?
—From "Didn't My Lord Deliver Daniel"

❦ Slaves wanted to be free: they understood the stories of deliverance and freedom in biblical tales that showed the Lord guiding and protecting Moses, and Daniel, and Jonah, and a host of minor and major prophets. It is a plaintive cry: Why shouldn't the Lord deliver every man, woman, and child from slavery? If God were preoccupied and moved too slowly, why shouldn't the enslaved disobey earthly laws and gain their own freedom? Why not try to make the dream of freedom come true?

Why not? Why not?

Whatever terrible conditions they were living under, slaves in the colonies up and down the Atlantic seaboard were able to flee from cruel masters and mistresses without violent action. The laws of the colonies recognized slavery as legal, but disaffected slaves consciously disobeyed the laws and conventions supporting slavery, knowing they would be punished if they were caught. These runaways were engaged in civil disobedience: "nonviolent opposition to a government policy or law by refusing to comply with it, on the grounds of conscience," according to Webster's. Whatever the problems the slaves faced—overwork, poor food, inadequate housing, the rape of women slaves, the breakup of family units resulting from sales—they understood that the system was wrong and degrading. They sought freedom as self-protection from the people and forces misusing them.

Because they lived in violent times, it was not unknown for slaves to murder their owners or to band together in an insurrection. Generally, though, they followed their consciences, regarded slavery as wrong, and attempted to escape bondage without doing bodily harm to anyone.

In the chapters that follow, we offer an account of African Americans and civil disobedience, charting the changes in philosophy over the centuries, from Socrates to Thoreau and Gandhi, and ending with the Montgomery, Alabama, civil rights movement led by Dr. Martin Luther King, Jr.

American slaves may not have known they were engaged in "civil disobedience," and they were certainly not the inventors of this course of action; throughout recorded history, individuals and groups have faced discriminatory laws and have searched for ways to oppose them. Certainly Socrates (469–399 B.C.) practiced civil disobedience. In his discussions with his fellow citizens he sought to expose the shallowness of their intellectual and moral beliefs. Ordered by authorities to halt his actions that they saw as traitorous and disruptive to civil order, he refused, accepted the death penalty, and drank hemlock. He believed that he was obeying God—a higher law—not men when he practiced his version of civil disobedience.

For centuries, students in schools and universities in the Western world have studied the classics and read Plato's *The Apology of Socrates*, thus gaining their own knowledge of the principles, defiance, and death of the philosopher and passing this knowledge from generation to generation. Studying the life and death of Socrates continued even in countries with despotic rulers who treated dissidents harshly. It was generally the elite who studied the classics, and it gave some of them an inkling of another worldview. The masses in those societies didn't read Plato on Socrates (perhaps didn't read at all), but they knew firsthand about oppressive laws and customs, and often found subversive ways to avoid or dispute them.

A larger number of people had read or heard what came to be known as the Holy Bible, containing the Old and New Testaments (1611). (The King James version was read by Protestants from colonial times until recently, when modern translations have appeared.) Some of the most famous examples of civil disobedience in the Old Testament are from Exodus, the Second Book of Moses. The king of Egypt, fearing the enslaved Israelites were multiplying too rapidly, decreed that midwives to Hebrew women should kill all male children. The midwives, fearing God (they too were following a higher law), refused, and male children were saved. Moses was born during this decree; his mother protected him for three months, and when she could not go on hiding him made an ark of bulrushes, placed the baby in it, and sent it down the river. The child was found by Pharaoh's daughter, who adopted him.

When Moses was an adult, God appeared to him in the burning bush, telling him to go to the king of Egypt with the message "Let my people go" (8:1). God predicted that Pharaoh would refuse, and God declared, "And I will stretch out my hand, and smite Egypt with all my wonders which I will do in the midst thereof: and after that he will let you go" (3:20). According to this account by Moses, God was surely the "higher law," and the Pharaoh had no real options; he was forced to let the children of Israel go. The tale was a powerful message of hope for slaves and for others oppressed for religious or political reasons.

After the exodus from Egypt, God gave Moses and his people the Ten Commandments, one of which—"Thou shalt not kill"—was interpreted literally by such religious groups as the Quakers, the Mennonites, and the Amish, placing them in conflict with civil governments everywhere that were all too ready to impose capital punishment or go to war. In late colonial times and in the nineteenth-century United States, small but influential sects of Quakers influenced the growing number of those followers of the "higher law" who opposed slavery.

Large numbers of religious people in the colonies and later in the newly established United States read and heard from pulpits the story of the civil disobedience of Jesus. The books of Matthew, Mark, Luke, and John in the King James version of the Bible contain accounts of the betrayal, capture, disobedience to religious and civil law, and execution of Jesus.

Jesus angered the priests by cleansing the temple of those who bought and sold there, and he cast out the moneychangers. When asked by the priest (Mark 14:61) if he were "the Christ, the Son of the Blessed," Jesus said, "I am." As Curtis Crawford notes in *Civil Disobedience: A Casebook*, "he disobeyed the law against blasphemy." The high priests refrained from having Jesus sent to his death on their own charges but delivered him into the hands of Pontius Pilate, the Roman procurator of Judaea, who asked, "Art thou the King of the Jews?" and Jesus responded (Matthew 27:11), "Thou sayest." As Crawford writes, "to the Romans as rulers of Palestine, the connotation of 'King of the Jews' was not some remote, problematical divine intervention, but the ever-present danger of rebellion against their occupation." Jesus was following a higher law, and the Romans executed him.

In the Sermon on the Mount, Jesus had previously enunciated two other concepts often used by civil disobedients. He is quoted in Matthew 5:38–39:

"Ye have heard that it hath been said, 'An eye for an eye and a tooth for a tooth.'

"But I say unto you, 'That ye resist not evil: but whosoever shall smite thee on thy right cheek, turn to him the other also.'"

Later in the sermon (Matthew 5:43–44) Jesus said,

"Ye have heard that it hath been said, 'Thou shalt love thy neighbor, and hate thine enemy.'

"But I say unto you, 'Love your enemies, bless them that curse you, do good to them that hate you, and pray for them which despitefully use you, and persecute you. . . .'"

These injunctions, special to Quakers, also appealed to nonviolent resisters and were reflected in the abolitionist movement in the United States. They were later used by Gandhi and King in their freedom movements.

The English political philosopher who was especially influential in the development of civil disobedience was John Locke (1632–1704), who argued that all people were servants of God and had natural rights to life, liberty, and property. In *Two Treatises on Civil Government* (1690), he argued the need for clearly stated laws and for impartial judges to interpret them, a set of circumstances that civil disobedients have often found missing.

Locke asserted that to ensure their rights, people must agree to the establishment of government. He recognized, however, that these established governments might violate their own laws and principles, giving rise to seemingly spontaneous eruptions of disobedience: "The people generally ill treated, and contrary to right, will be ready upon any occasion to ease themselves of a burden that sits heavy upon them." Locke, though, does not call for nonviolence. What he does offer is a philosophic rationale for disobedience, which especially influenced the Declaration of Independence (1776), written primarily by Thomas Jefferson but with revisions and amendments before final adoption.

That Declaration was a revolutionary document, announcing, "We hold these truths to be self-evident, that all men are created equal, that they are endowed by their Creator with certain unalienable Rights, that among these are Life, Liberty, and the pursuit of Happiness." Protecting the rights of blacks, however, was opposed by many Southern delegates to the convention who were slaveholders or sympathetic to slavery, and passages favorable to slaves were edited out before the final adoption. These charges against George III were excluded: "He has waged cruel war against human nature itself, violating its most sacred rights of life and liberty in the persons of a distant people who never offended him, captivating and carrying them into slavery in another hemisphere, or to incur miserable death in their transportation thither." Southerners insisted that all such sentiments be deleted. While they led the way on this issue, in truth in 1776 there were few leaders in any of the colonies who were interested in protecting the rights of blacks. Most blacks and abolitionists who later cited the

Declaration of Independence to support their causes were not aware of this deletion. But they could and did read the document literally, seeing it as applying to all people.

The Constitution of the United States, ratified in 1788, recognized slavery and thereby gave slaveowners the force of law as they defended the "peculiar institution." The Constitution and the Bill of Rights, its first ten amendments, protected many rights of white Americans but offered no protection for blacks.

In many practical ways, however, abolitionists who opposed slavery began to help escaping fugitives and to propagandize for emancipation. Their activities met with fierce opposition from Southern slaveholders and their apologists, many of whom were bankers and merchants in the North. It was in this environment that Henry David Thoreau (1817–1862) of Concord, Massachusetts, wrote his essay "Civil Disobedience" (also called "Resistance to Civil Government"), first offered as a lecture in 1848 and published in 1849. Thoreau's mother, Cynthia, was a local leader in the abolitionist movement. Abolitionist speakers who came to Concord often stayed at the Thoreau house, and the Thoreau family read the abolitionist newspapers and worked with those who helped escaping slaves. We know that Thoreau was personally involved in assisting fugitives. His essay was also a response to the Mexican War (1846–1848), for he and many others believed that the U.S. war against Mexico was being waged to open up additional territories to slavery.

As an act of defiance, Thoreau refused to pay his poll tax, was jailed for one night, and was angered when his tax was paid, probably by a family member. He then wrote his essay about a government gone awry in supporting slavery and about the principled act of going to jail for breaking the law. An independent man, he acted alone, not waiting for others to

Henry David Thoreau wrote his essay "Civil
Disobedience" in 1848. *(Concord Free Public Library)*

join his protest. Many of his sentences in "Civil Disobedience"
are memorable:

". . . To speak practically and as a citizen, unlike those who
call themselves no-government men, I ask for, not at once no
government, but *at once* a better government."

"The mass of men serve the State thus, not as men mainly,
but as machines, with their bodies."

"Under a government which imprisons any unjustly, the
true place for a just man is also a prison."

Thoreau readily accepted punishment—a jail sentence—for
his disobedience. This element of his approach was adopted by
Gandhi, King, and many others who followed him.

Thoreau's entire essay became important to Mohandas K. Gandhi (1869–1948) in developing a plan of noncooperation and civil disobedience, first to help Indian "coolies" in South Africa and then to win independence from British rule for his home country India. Thoreau had acted alone, but Gandhi developed a mass movement, one that would throw sand in the machinery of government by filling the jails with civil disobedients. Gandhi's civil disobedience movement certainly owed much to Hindu religion and culture, with its emphasis on the sacredness of all life, but in the early stages of its development he was influenced by Thoreau. Thoreau's essay "Civil Disobedience" made its way to Gandhi in South Africa and India and later returned to the segregated South of the United States. There Dr. Martin Luther King, Jr. (1929–1968), adopted the Gandhian methods of nonviolent resistance.

Dr. King, reacting to the massive denial of civil rights to blacks, owed intellectual and philosophical debts to the Christian religion—he was a Baptist minister—and to Thoreau and Gandhi. Like Gandhi, he worked to achieve episodes of mass civil disobedience. From his religion, especially the Sermon on the Mount, he argued that all men are brothers and that love "can hold this broken community together. When I am commanded to love, I am commanded to restore community," he wrote in *Stride Toward Freedom*, "to resist injustice, and to meet the needs of my brothers."

The chapters on Gandhi and Dr. King are concerned with the less familiar early formulation of their concepts and their practice of civil disobedience, and make only passing reference to their later struggles, which have been well documented elsewhere.

Nonviolence was at times met with violence, and that too is part of our story. Whites and blacks who helped black civil disobedients are also part of this story, as are whites who treated blacks inhumanely and unjustly, often precipitating acts of civil disobedience.

In the last paragraph of "Civil Disobedience," Thoreau wrote, "I please myself with imagining a State at last which can afford to be just to all men. . . ."

Why not every man?

CHAPTER

1

SLAVERY AND

CIVIL DISOBEDIENCE FROM

COLONIAL TIMES TO 1830

No more auction block for me,
No more, no more,
No more auction block for me,
Many thousand gone.
—From "Many Thousand Gone"

❧ The twenty Africans who were aboard a Dutch frigate that landed in Jamestown, Virginia, in 1619 were not considered slaves. Instead they were called indentured servants, and like whites in the same condition they were to be given an allotment of land after they had served the terms of their indenture. As more labor was needed for the growing of tobacco, which sold at high prices in Europe, American colonists decided by 1640 that indentured black servants should become slaves in perpetuity. This proposed change in status was put into effect slowly, and as late as 1651 some black indentured servants were freed and given land. Blacks as indentured servants in the decades after 1619 were certainly in an awkward situation: not slaves, not really free, subject to enslavement with few means of protest. Slowly, slavery became recognized by statute, and movement in this direction went on for a generation. In 1662 the House of Burgesses in Virginia declared that children should follow the condition of their mothers, not their fathers, thus making slave birthrates important to slave masters who fathered children in the slave quarters. In 1667 slaves were allowed to be baptized in the Christian faith, but baptism did not confer freedom on them.

The Atlantic slave trade brought thousands of slaves to Virginia, and by 1756 there were 120,156 blacks and 173,316 whites in the colony. Whites were becoming more fearful of plots and organized insurrections against the owners of slaves. A comprehensive slave code, drawing on those developed in the Caribbean islands, was adopted in Virginia: Slaves could leave the plantation only with the permission of their owners. Slaves found outside the plantation without a permit were taken back to their owners. Slaves who murdered or raped were hanged; others guilty of major crimes were to be given sixty lashes. Slaves who committed minor crimes might be whipped or branded. Slaves could not legally marry, could not testify against whites in a court of law, and could not congregate in large numbers. Other colonies adopted similar codes.

The largest numbers of slaves were held in the tobacco-growing areas of Virginia, Maryland, and North Carolina and in the rice-growing areas of South Carolina. Cotton did not become a commercial crop until the cotton gin was invented by Eli Whitney in 1793 and after new lands were opened in the Deep South.

Slaves were not allowed in Georgia when that colony was established in 1733, but the prohibition was lifted in 1750, after which slavery grew rapidly. The Georgia slave code of 1755 was highly restrictive: a white chaperone had to be in attendance if more than seven slaves were meeting. It was forbidden to teach slaves to read or write. Blacks, though, were required to serve in the militia and were armed when carrying out official duties. Georgia slaveowners greatly feared slave insurrections, a fear that was largely unjustified, for the slaves had a safety valve: if they were dissatisfied or treated badly, maroons, as fugitives were called, could (and did) declare disobedience and flee to Spanish Florida, often to live with Indians.

In the Middle Colonies, the Dutch slaves in New Netherland lived under a less oppressive slave code. In 1664, however, when the English took over from the Dutch, conditions for slaves began to deteriorate. In 1706 the colony passed a law declaring that the baptism of slaves did not convey freedom to them, and that slaves could not give legal testimony against freemen. By 1715 the numbers of New York slaves attempting to escape to Canada must have been significant, for new legislation called for the execution of slaves who journeyed forty miles north of Albany "upon the oath of two credible witnesses." After bloody slave insurrections in 1712 and 1741, New York City enacted further oppressive laws against blacks.

The English also actively encouraged the growth of slavery in New Jersey. But in Pennsylvania, the home of many Quakers (the Society of Friends) with their belief in nonviolence, slaves were better treated than in many other colonies. By 1784 the Quakers had prohibited slavery altogether. Those Quakers who owned slaves were persuaded to emancipate them, or the slaveowners were themselves disowned by the Friends. John Hope Franklin and Alfred Moss, in *From Slavery to Freedom*, are correct in asserting, "Slavery was never really successful in the Middle colonies." The Dutch, Swedish, and German farmers preferred to do their own work, and the Quaker influence, especially in Pennsylvania, was effectively responsible for the moral and ethical scruples against holding blacks in bondage.

In New England, as Franklin and Moss argue, the "primary interest in slavery was in the trade of blacks." But slaves were living there as early as 1638 when several were brought into Boston. In 1700 the population of the New England colonies was approximately ninety thousand, only a thousand of whom were blacks. The numbers of slaves grew more rapidly in the eighteenth century, and Connecticut and Rhode Island acquired significant slave populations, though the numbers throughout New England remained small. There were occasional rebellions, and the colonies did enact less restrictive slave codes than those in the South. New Englanders, however, were far from humanitarian in their treatment of slaves, and Franklin and Moss note that they "held a firm hand on the institution and gave little consideration to the small minority that argued for the freedom of the slaves."

Some slaves in the New England colonies did not accept servitude and ran away to other colonies. In 1643 the New England Confederation of Plymouth, Massachusetts, Connecticut, and New Haven, in its Articles of Confederation, addressed the problem: "If any servant runn away from his master into any other of these confederated Jurisdiccons, That in such cases upon the Certyficate of one Majistrate in the Jurisdiccon out of which the said servant fled, or upon other due proofs, the said servant shall be delivered either to his Master or any other that pursues and brings such Certificate or proofe." With minor changes, similar wording was used in America for the next two hundred years, culminating in the Fugitive Slave Act of 1850.

Several of the patterns of escape used by fugitive slaves were set before the American Revolution. Some slaves sought freedom by mingling with free blacks; others joined Indian tribes. Others simply vanished, and owners searched for them, often with armed men and dogs, and advertised for the return of their escaped slaves.

On August 11, 1761, George Washington advertised that four of his slaves had escaped. One of those escapees had spent years around Williamsburg, and Washington suspected he might have returned there, where there were several blacks known to help fugitives escape. An overseer on one of the plantations belonging to Martha Custis Washington wrote that it would do no good to put shackles on slaves in the Williamsburg area, for "the negro Blacksmiths would soon file them off."

Captured runaway slaves were often sold. George Washington was hardly a benevolent master, as Henry Wiencek shows in *An Imperfect God*. After a slave named Tom belonging to Washington escaped, Washington paid two pounds sterling in expenses for the recovery of the slave and promptly put him out for sale. Tom was not sold "down the river" into the Deep South, for that was a largely nineteenth-century practice for disposing of troublesome or overstocked slaves. Tom was sold into the Caribbean.

Washington wrote on July 2, 1766, to the captain of the *Swift*, ready to sail to the Caribbean islands: "With this Letter comes a negro (Tom) which I beg the favor of you to sell. . . ." Washington did not set a price in money for the sale; instead he requested a hogshead of molasses, a hogshead of rum, a barrel of limes "if good and Cheap," ten pounds of tamarinds, ten pounds of sweetmeats, "And the residue, much or little, in good old Spirits."

In his letter to the captain about Tom, Washington cast himself as an honest man. He admitted that Tom was a "Rogue & Runaway," but his roguishness was not "remarkable" and his runaway propensities "never practised . . . till of late." In fact, Washington testified to Tom's excellent qualities; he was "healthy, strong, and good at the Hoe." Then Washington moved away from truthtelling, insisting that "the whole neighborhood" could testify to Tom's fine qualities. It is highly unlikely that the entire neighborhood around Mount Vernon knew Tom, and certainly buyers in Barbados or Jamaica who might consider purchasing Tom could not easily discover how Washington's neighbors regarded the "Rogue and Runaway" who had declared civil disobedience when he absconded.

Henry Wiencek, in his magisterial *An Imperfect God*, places Washington in an even harsher light regarding the sale of Tom: "The West Indies plantations were disease-ridden pest holes, the preferred dumping ground for troublesome mainland slaves. Washington had visited Barbados and knew the horrors of the work-them-to-death sugarcane plantations there." Washington sold other slaves to the island and threatened still others with the same fate.

During the Colonial period and later, some slaves disappeared overnight or for a few days while visiting wives and children or lovers on a nearby plantation. Such slaves were almost always peaceful, but they were deliberately disobeying the rule of the master and the slave code of the colony. Slaves who "layed out"—disappeared for an extended period of time—were often guilty of looting and pilfering in order to survive. They were undoubtedly disciplined more harshly than those who were away for a short time visiting spouses and children.

In addition to the maroons in Spanish Florida, there were similar settlements in the colonies. Many maroons had fled harsh punishments and settled in isolated woods and swamps. They were generally peaceful civil disobedients, but they sometimes resorted to petty theft in order to continue living in their remote areas. Were they following the "higher law" in seeking freedom yet "liberating" foodstuffs and household items? A desire for freedom drove them to flight and to theft.

The best-known justification for such action is to be found not in the Colonial period but in Frederick Douglass's only work of fiction, "The Heroic Slave" (1853). The escaped slave Madison Washington, the central character, had hidden in a forest for several years before a fire forced him out, and he headed for Canada, stealing food along the way in order to survive. He justified his actions to a sympathetic white man who aided him: "Your moral code may differ from mine, as your customs and usages are different. The fact is, sir, during my flight, I felt myself robbed by society of all my just rights; that I was in an enemy's land, who sought both my life and my liberty. They transformed me into a brute; made merchandise of my body, and for the purposes of my flight, turned day into night,—and guided by my own necessities, and in contempt of their conventionalities, I did not scruple to take bread where I could get it." Conventional religious people and law-and-order adherents in the seventeenth, eighteenth, and nineteenth centuries, when slavery was a divisive force in American society, would have had problems with such reasoning.

By the end of the Colonial period, patterns of slavery were well established. Masters like to boast that their "servants" were docile and content. At the same time the masters relied upon the slave codes and punishments to break the spirit of runaways, recalcitrants, and "criminals." As Franklin and

Moss note, "With the sheriff, the courts, and even the slaveless whites on their sides, the masters should have experienced no difficulty in maintaining peace among their slaves."

In fact the masters had been perpetuating a myth. The spirit of many blacks was not broken. Some revolted. Others murdered their owners, or raided plantation storerooms, or destroyed farm property such as hoes and plows. Some killed or maimed farm animals. Most of the slaves, when they protested, were peaceful in their disobedience: they malingered, deliberately misunderstood directions or orders, or ran away, undeterred by threats, whippings, and a variety of cruel punishments from authority figures.

Some Quakers, such as John Woolman (1720–1772), an itinerant preacher, protested the institution of slavery altogether. He came to believe "slave keeping to be a practice inconsistent with the Christian religion." A man of conscience, he often spoke out against slavery. The philosopher A. N. Whitehead called Woolman the "first Apostle of human freedom." Benjamin Franklin and Dr. Benjamin Rush also urged the freeing of slaves, but their views were mostly ignored.

The high import duties imposed against the colonies in the 1760s and early 1770s were important reasons for the growing resistance to what was thought to be British tyranny. The British did not discern the depth of revolutionary feeling in the colonies expressed by the Boston Tea Party and other protests. Skirmishes began when Minutemen in Concord and Lexington, Massachusetts, clashed with British troops in April 1775. These skirmishes continued until 1776, when the colonies declared their independence on July 4. Their Declaration, with its ringing words about human freedom, did not really apply to blacks, though a literal interpretation could make it seem so. James Forten, a free black who was a successful businessman, wrote in 1813 in *A Series of Letters by a Man of Color:* "We hold this truth to be self-evident, that God created all men equal, is one of the most prominent features in the Declaration of Independence, and in that glorious fabric of collected wisdom of our noble Constitution." The optimistic Forten was mistaken, for the Constitution, even more than the Declaration of Independence, failed to protect the rights of blacks.

Ironically, thousands of slaves during the Revolutionary War became free by joining British forces. By such action they were declaring civil disobedience against slaveholders and the Continental Congress. General George Washington ordered on November 12, 1775, that blacks, free or slave, were not to be enlisted in the army. A few days earlier, on November 7, Lord Dunmore, the British governor of Virginia, proclaimed, "I do hereby . . . declare all indentured servants, Negroes, or others (appertaining to rebels) free, that are able and willing to bear arms, they joining his Majesty's troops, as soon as may be, for the more speedily reducing the Colony to a proper dignity." The offer was appealing to slaves. Jefferson estimated in 1778 that thirty thousand slaves had run away in Virginia. Not all of them had joined the British forces, of course, for in the confusion of wartime, slaves could more easily disappear without serving in the British army or navy. Georgia is said to have lost three-quarters of its slaves during the war. These slaves were declaring civil disobedience against their owners and against the newly forming government of what was to become the United States.

General Washington soon reversed his earlier policy and on December 31, 1775, allowed the enlistment of free blacks. About five thousand blacks, most of them from Northern states, served in the Revolutionary army, but Washington's order did not allow slaves to serve in exchange for freedom. In fact several Northern colonies had allowed slaves to enlist in the Revolutionary forces before Washington's order of December 31. Those enlisting slaves and the state officials who sanctioned their enlistment were all civil disobedients. These Northern slaves who enlisted were soon to be free, for many of the Northern states were ready to begin abolishing slavery.

With the end of the war, a convention drawing up the Constitution of the United States set the stage for decades of civil disobedience movements by blacks and whites opposing the institution of slavery. Gouverneur Morris of New York, a delegate to the convention, said slavery "was the curse of heaven on the states where it prevailed. . . ." His views did not prevail.

Anti-slavery advocates and revolutionaries who believed in the rights of all mankind fought to keep slavery from being codified in the Constitution, but they failed. Slavery remained in place, but a date was set for ending the slave trade. In addition, Article I, Section 2.3 of the Constitution reads: "Representatives and direct Taxes shall be apportioned among the several States which may be included within this Union, according to their respective numbers, which shall be determined by adding to the whole number of free persons, including those bound to service for a term of years, and excluding Indians not taxed, three-fifths of all other persons." In other words, a slave was now to be counted for political purposes as three-fifths of a person.

The words "slaves" and "slavery" were not used in the Constitution, hiding the reality that slavery was for a lifetime. The language of the Constitution in this section is bland, deceptive to the unwary, and protective of pro-slavery rights.

That three-fifths rule had been debated heatedly. Gouverneur Morris asked pointed questions: "Upon what principle is it that the slaves shall be computed in the representation?

Are they men? Then make them citizens and let them vote. Are they property? Why then is no other property included? The houses in [Philadelphia] are worth more than all the wretched slaves which cover the rice swamps of South Carolina."

This three-fifths compromise—Southerners had argued for a total count of slaves—allowed the Southern states, where most of the slaves resided, to count every slave as three-fifths of a person in establishing the number of members of the House of Representatives, and it also influenced representation in the Electoral College. Garry Wills quotes from the *Columbian Sentinel* of December 24, 1800, that slaves "had no more will in the matter than 'New England horses, cows, and oxen.'"

This three-fifths flaw in the Constitution, Wills writes, "gave a key electoral tool for maintaining slavery against a majority of white voters. . . ." The rule became a constant irritant, an invitation to disobedience in the following decades as supporters of the slaves' rights for freedom looked for ways to attack pro-slavery positions.

One of Thomas Jefferson's political rivals, writing directly about rumors that Jefferson had children with his slave Sally Hemings, suggested that with five of these mulatto children Jefferson would accumulate three more votes:

Great men can never lack supporters
Who manufacture their own voters.

A product of many compromises, including the three-fifths rule, the Constitution was ratified in 1788. Slavery continued to be legal, and whites in the South, with the three-fifths rule in place, had new powers to defend it.

Several events at the close of the eighteenth century encouraged discontent among slaves and optimism among their supporters. The French Revolution that began in 1789 was bloody, and slaves and their masters recognized that downtrodden people could overthrow established rule. Slaves, often cruelly treated, could understand, even sympathize, with the hatred being directed at French aristocrats. They would agree with the French revolutionaries on the possibilities of Liberty, Equality, and Fraternity. Slave revolts had already taken place, usually on a minor scale, in the colonies, but the French Revolution pointed the way to violent acts as opposed to the usual nonviolence of fugitive slaves. Did slaves learn about the French Revolution? Most could not read, but apparently they did hear accounts of what was happening in France.

Another important event occurred on the Caribbean island of Saint Domingue (now Haiti), where blacks in that French possession demanded the same freedoms being won by the French revolutionists. The revolt was led by Toussaint L'Ouverture from 1794 to 1800, when he was captured by the French. Haiti, in revolt, was not subdued. W. E. B. Du Bois said of the Haitian leader and his influence: "He rose to leadership through a bloody terror, which contrived a Negro 'problem' for the Western Hemisphere, intensified and defined the anti-slavery movement, became one of the causes . . . which led Napoleon to sell Louisiana for a song, and finally, through the interworking of all these effects, rendered more certain the final prohibition of the slave-trade by the United States in 1807." Most slaves in the colonies and in the early years of the United States declared their civil disobedience by the solitary act of running away, liberating only themselves. L'Ouverture's rebellion, on the other hand, proved that a large-scale uprising could be carried out close to the shores of the United States, thus encouraging those who wanted to use violence to end slavery.

But the other effect of the violent revolution in Haiti is that Quakers and other abolitionist groups were emboldened to use the legislative process to end the slave trade. Congress equivocated about plans to change the constitutional ban against the importation of slaves, and the Quakers and the Pennsylvania Abolition Society continued their protests over several years. When efforts to change that provision of the Constitution failed, slaves could no longer be brought into the United States legally after the last day of 1807, but some illegal importation by ship continued.

Qualms about slaveholding had grown in several Northern states out of religious objections, abolitionist agitation, and the growth of the spirit of freedom. Most persuasive, perhaps, the institution of slavery had become unprofitable in the North, though the slave trade remained profitable. While the reasons were varied and compelling, in just over a quarter of a century these Northern states began to abolish slavery:

1777, Vermont
1780, Pennsylvania (began gradual abolition)
1783, Massachusetts and New Hampshire
1784, Rhode Island and Connecticut (began gradual abolition)
1799, New York (began gradual abolition)
1804, New Jersey (began gradual aboliton)

These free states gave rise to a problem of consequence: they provided a haven for runaway slaves. To address this issue, Congress in 1793 passed the Fugitive Slave Law, the terms of which were similar to the 1643 article adopted by the New England Confederation of Plymouth, Massachusetts, Connecticut, and New Haven. According to the 1793 law, an owner or agent could recapture a fugitive slave, take him or

her before a judge or commissioner, and certify that the accused person was a slave. That done, the slave could be returned to the area from which he or she had fled and to the
rightful owner. A fine of $500 could be levied against anyone
rescuing or harboring a slave.

Strangely enough, given the power of the South in Congress, the Fugitive Slave Act of 1793 was little enforced at a
time when abolitionist activity was growing and more slaves
were taking leave of their masters. The Quaker activist Isaac
Hopper (1771?–1852) developed "underground" routes for
escaping slaves as early as 1787. Hopper's activities—clearly
in the mode of civil disobedience—were known to the public,
but most Quakers and other abolitionists worked secretly.

While Hopper's activities were often illegal, he also worked
within the law. He helped raise funds to purchase fugitive
slaves after they had escaped. Many other abolitionists in the
late eighteenth and nineteenth centuries until the time of the
Civil War also raised money to purchase escapees and members of their families still in servitude. Paying to free slaves
posed ethical problems for some abolitionists; many of them
felt it wrong to compensate slaveholders and continued to defy
the Fugitive Slave Act.

Some radical civil disobedients such as the white John Fairfield, an acquaintance of the Quaker Underground "conductor" Levi Coffin, made excursions into the South in the years
preceding the Civil War to steal family members of escaped
slaves and reunite them in the North or in Canada. Fairfield
actively broke the law for the freedom of slaves. He told Coffin, "I would steal all the slaves in Virginia if I could." Coffin
found himself in an ethical dilemma, for it was his practice to
help slaves only after they had escaped. He did not agree with
Fairfield's principles, but he helped the slaves Fairfield rescued.

Two letters by George Washington in 1786 express his frustration at the growing abolitionist movement. He wrote on May 12 about a slave belonging to a man in Alexandria, Virginia, who had escaped to Philadelphia, and "whom a society of Quakers in the city, formed for such purposes, have attempted to liberate." Later that year, on November 20, he wrote that he had sent a slave to William Drayton, under the care of an overseer, and the slave had escaped. Washington wrote, "The gentleman to whose care I sent him has promised every endeavor to apprehend him, but it is not easy to do this, when there are numbers who would rather facilitate the escape of slaves than apprehend them when runaways."

What Washington was referring to was the Underground Railroad, though it had not yet been named. Just when that term came into use is open to question, but in 1831 a slave named Tice Davids swam across the Ohio, landing near Ripley, Ohio. After his master searched for him unsuccessfully, he remarked that the "nigger must have gone off on an underground road."

The Chicago *Western Citizen*, an abolitionist paper, printed the following account in its December 23, 1842, issue: An escaped slave who returned South and was tortured said of his escapade, "the abolitionists had a *railroad under ground* and that he started for it; but when he got there the 'trap door' was *shut*."

There are other stories about the term Underground Railroad, perhaps many of them apocryphal, but there was indeed a largely secret, loosely organized group of people, blacks and whites, who helped fleeing slaves, moving them from one "conductor" to another until they were in a safe area.

After steam-engine trains were introduced in the United States in 1830, those involved in helping escaped slaves began

to adopt train terminology: "passenger," "depot" or "station," and "conductor." All the participants in Underground
Railroad activities were civil disobedients. Quakers were un-
armed, though some runaways and conductors did carry
knives or sticks or guns for self-protection.

Certainly not all the abolitionists in the early nineteenth
century were Quakers. The white man John Rankin, born in
east Tennessee in 1793, was a Presbyterian minister. His life
and career have been brilliantly recreated by Ann Hagedorn in
Beyond the River. A graduate of Washington College in
Jonesboro, Tennessee, in 1816, Rankin supported the Manumission Society of Tennessee. The Abingdon Presbytery in his
part of the state looked on him "with suspicion and distrust
because of his frequent expression of opposition to slavery." In
his early abolitionist days, Reverend Rankin tried to convince
owners to free their slaves, but as pro-slavery beliefs developed
more strongly in that area he was told in 1817 that he should
leave the state if he wished to oppose slavery.

Rankin, his wife, and infant son left Tennessee and settled
for four years in Kentucky, where he preached and worked for
the Kentucky Abolitionist Society. His anti-slavery activities
were conducted within the law. He started a school for slaves,
but since under Kentucky law teaching slaves to read was forbidden, he did not use books but rather lectured to his students. His attempts to be law-abiding did not succeed.
Pro-slavery elements in the community objected to his activities, broke into the schoolhouse, and drove the students out.
Rankin found another place to meet, but when the students
left after a teaching session, the mob set upon them with clubs.
The slaves were too frightened to continue, and Rankin was
forced to close his school.

In 1821 he moved his family to Ripley, Ohio, on the Ohio
River, where he became a leading abolitionist, disobeying the

Fugitive Slave Act several thousand times. He was a known abolitionist, actively sought out by escaping slaves and repeatedly threatened by supporters of slavery. He and his sons often carried guns for self-protection.

The abolitionist William Still of Philadelphia, a free black man, was also a Presbyterian, active in church affairs. Like Rankin and Coffin, he was an active civil disobedient, assisting several thousand fleeing slaves. He wrote an excellent account of his activities as a conductor in *The Underground Rail Road*.

Not all abolitionists were conventionally religious. Henry David Thoreau, the Transcendental naturalist writer now best remembered for his book *Walden* and his essay "Civil Disobedience," is well known for his individualism. He distrusted most institutions and signed off from the church, for he did not attend services and saw no reason to support the minister.

As a young man, the Harvard-educated Thoreau became a close follower of Ralph Waldo Emerson (1803–1882), whose *Nature* was a revelation to him, providing an important guide for his own studies. In the sterile atmosphere of rationalist Unitarian religion then prominent in New England, he found in *Nature* an appealing account of mysticism: "Standing on the bare ground,—my head bathed by the blithe air, and uplifted into infinite space,—all mean egotism vanishes. I become a transparent eye-ball. I am nothing. I see all. The currents of the Universal Being circulate through me; I am part or particle of God."

Thoreau, also interested in mysticism, followed Emerson in reading oriental texts. He made a special study of the *Bhagavad Gita* and other Hindu works.

There was a hint of asceticism in Thoreau's life, and at times he practiced a form of mystical contemplation. He wrote his friend H. G. O. Blake in 1849, quoting Hindu scriptures first: "The yogi, absorbed in contemplation, contributes in his

degree to creation; he breathes a divine perfume, he hears
wonderful things. Divine forms traverse him without tearing
him, and, united to the nature which is proper to him, he goes,
he acts as animating original matter."

Thoreau then added: "To some extent, and at rare inter-
vals, even I am a yogi."

Thoreau's praise of the *Bhagavad Gita* reflects its impact
upon him: "The reader is nowhere raised into and sustained in
a higher, purer, or rarer reason. . . ." This Hindu religious text
contains the dialogue of Krishna, God incarnate as a chario-
teer, and Arjuna, the strong fighter, just before a great battle.
Arjuna did not wish to fight a fratricidal war, did not want to
become an instrument of death. Krishna urged him to put
aside his doubts. He told him that souls were without beginning or end, that there was no death in battle, for the soul
changes the outward body for another. Arjuna should do his
duty and go into battle. This was the way of Action. There was
also another way—Contemplation—that is, to become a yogi,
who would "cast off all desires" and would have "no thought
of a *Mine* or an *I*. . . ."

In *Walden*, Thoreau described a yogilike experiment:
"Sometimes, in a summer morning, having taken my accustomed bath, I sat in my sunny doorway from sunrise till noon,
rapt in a revery, amidst the pines and hickories and sumachs,
in undisturbed solitude and stillness, . . . until by the sun
falling in my west window, or the noise of some traveller's
wagon on the distant highway, I was reminded of the lapse of
time. I grew in those seasons like corn in the night. . . . I realized what the Orientals mean by contemplation and the for-
saking of works."

When Thoreau was studying nature, writing, lecturing,
and helping escaped slaves, he was a man of action; at other

times he was a mystic. He combined the active and contemplative lives. The conflict over slavery drew him away, at least for short periods of time, from his nature studies and his experiences as a mystic into becoming an actor in the abolitionist drama. He supported abolitionist causes and is known to have helped escaping slaves, and in "Civil Disobedience," "Slavery in Massachusetts," and other essays he was an active man on the urgent issue of his time. It is not surprising that Gandhi, the Hindu politician and holy man, found much to admire in Thoreau's life and works.

When the Louisiana Purchase of 1803 opened up vast new areas for the growing of sugar cane and cotton, pro-slavery sentiments flourished throughout the South. Manumission societies were generally forced out of the region but grew in the North. While they were still in the South, escaping slaves were largely on their own, except for what help they might receive from other slaves, free blacks, and the occasional abolitionist whose identity and activities were hidden. Once out of the South, escaping slaves could expect more assistance, but they were also in great danger of being captured by slave catchers.

As the national debate over slavery intensified, the question of whether to admit Missouri as a slave or a free state erupted in Congress. The Missouri Compromise of 1820 let the pro-slavery element claim Missouri, but Maine was to enter as a free state, and slavery was banned north of the 36° 30' line of latitude in the Louisiana territory. That compromise proved to be unsatisfactory to both pro- and anti-slavery groups, for other states were forming, and the battles over their admission as free or slave states were often fierce.

Abolitionist publications, many favoring nonviolence and civil disobedience (though that term was not then used), began to appear, but at first they were limited in appeal. Benjamin

Lundy (1789–1839), from a Quaker family, founded the anti-slavery periodical *Philanthropist* in 1819 and *Genius of Universal Emancipation* in 1821. William Lloyd Garrison (1805–1879), an associate editor of the *Genius* in 1829, two years later founded the *Liberator* in Boston. It was published until 1865. The *National Anti-Slavery Standard* was published in New York and the abolitionist *Western Messenger* in Chicago. After the black abolitionist Frederick Douglass broke with Garrison, he began publishing the *North Star* in 1847.

Blacks were also busy writing and publishing papers, books, and pamphlets. David Ruggles (1810–1849), a free black man, had his own press and from 1838 to 1841 published *Mirror of Liberty*, dealing with the activities of the New York Vigilance Committee, kidnappings of free blacks and the resultant court cases, and the activities of black organizations. He also published major pamphlets such as the feminist work *The Abrogation of the Seventh Commandment by the American Churches*. He argued that Southern women stood by passively while their husbands fathered mulatto children born as slaves. He urged Northern women to shun Southern women who brought their slaves on visits to free states and to close their churches to them.

Frederick Douglass, the most influential of the black abolitionists, was known for his forceful autobiographies and his stirring speeches; he had the voice and delivery of a master orator. His *North Star* later became *Frederick Douglass' Weekly*.

David Walker (1796 or 1797–1830), a free black, was involved in planning the periodical *Freedom's Journal* in 1817 and then *Rights for All*, serving as agent for both. In 1829 he published the pamphlet *David Walker's Appeal*, a militant work that incited slaves to insurrection.

Henry Highland Garnet (1815–1882), born a slave, escaped bondage when he was nine. He became a Presbyterian minister and a militant abolitionist whose views were rejected by nonviolent followers of Garrison. Adhering to precepts *in David Walker's Appeal*, he urged slaves to win freedom through violent rebellion.

There were many other abolitionist voices, some urging nonresistance, others violence. Slavery and racial segregation were defended, North and South, for economic, political, or social reasons. While we concentrate on nonviolent civil disobedience in the pages to follow, violence and threats of violence are often present in the ensuing events.

11

ABOLITIONISTS, 1830–1861

Foller the drinkin' gou'd
Foller the drinkin' gou'd
For the ole man say,
"Foller the drinkin' gou'd."
—From "Follow the Drinkin' Gou'd"*

🌱 Four major groups contributed to the nonviolent abolitionist activities in the three decades preceding the Civil War.
Individual conductors, both black and white, in slave and free
states, worked quietly to help escaping slaves. This group included Thoreau, who wrote the major document advocating
civil disobedience, though that essay was not widely read or
understood during his lifetime.

Quakers (the Society of Friends), though a small religious
group, included many members who were sympathetic to the
abolitionist cause but also some orthodox Quakers who
played no role in helping free the enslaved. Quakers such as
Levi Coffin and Isaac Hopper were known for their activism,
and a larger number worked behind the scenes as conductors.

*Follow the celestial Big Dipper north to freedom.

Followers of William Lloyd Garrison, known as Garrisonians, tended to be reformers on a large scale, espousing tem-
perance and the rights of women as well as the abolition of
slavery. Garrison and his followers were strident in advocating
the abolition of slavery, often making enemies and alienating
even some among those who sympathized with their positions.

Garrison believed the Constitution to be an iniquitous document. Abandoning any hope of achieving the emancipation
of slaves through political activity, he hoped to win supporters
to the cause through moral suasion. Most Garrisonians did
not vote and would not hold political office. Noting that most
churches actively or passively accepted slavery, they dissoci-
ated themselves from these churches. Individual conductors,
free blacks, and Quakers were often Garrisonians and subscribed to the *Liberator*, the paper that Garrison edited.

An offshoot of the Garrisonian movement was the Nonresistance Society, made up largely of Quakers and religious
New Englanders from evangelical churches. As Carleton
Mabee has written in *Black Freedom*, most of the Nonresistance members agreed on principles deriving from the New
Testament: "(1) not resisting evil with evil (hence the misleading term 'nonresistant'), (2) positive resistance to evil with
good, (3) obedience to government in general but disobedience
to specific unjust laws, with meek acceptance of any resulting
punishment, (4) not so much inflicting suffering on others, as
taking suffering on oneself, (5) not so much changing outward
situations—which acting through government is likely to do—
as fundamentally changing individual motivation."

Many of these principles appealed to Thoreau, but as an
individualist he rethought and restated some of those which
undoubtedly seemed to him overtly Christian. Leo Tolstoy was
particularly impressed with the Nonresistants. Later, Gandhi

and King, from a variety of sources, developed policies closely parallel to these five principles.

Another quiet group was the Tappanites, encouraged by the wealthy white merchants Lewis and Arthur Tappan. Unlike the Garrisonians, the Tappanites believed in working with the existing political parties. They included many members from Presbyterian and Congregational churches. They seemed quieter because they were less strident than the Garrisonians. They were not total Nonresistants and would use force for self-protection if necessary.

Frederick Douglass does not fit easily (or for very long) into any of these groups. He began his abolitionist career after escaping from bondage, became a Garrisonian, then broke with Garrison and founded his own abolitionist publication, *The North Star*. He came to believe that it was possible to work within the system. As the conflict over slavery grew, he turned more to the belief that violence would be necessary to overthrow slavery.

Thoreau accepted ideas and principles from the Garrisonians and the Nonresistants. He was a quiet conductor, but by the close of the 1850s he came to feel a pull toward violence, speaking and writing favorably about John Brown and his raid at Harpers Ferry.

Some individuals who helped slaves escape acted only as circumstances dictated. Such was the case of the woman who helped Lear Green.

The eighteen-year-old slave Lear Green from Baltimore was engaged to William Adams, a black barber who also worked in taverns opening oysters. Green did not wish to live in a slave state after her marriage, and decided to flee. She was helped by her future mother-in-law, a free black living in New York. Green decided to ship herself to Philadelphia in a large

To flee a slave state, eighteen-year-old Lear Green shipped herself from Baltimore to Philadelphia in a large chest.

chest, outfitted with a quilt, pillow, clothes, food, and water. After she climbed into the chest, it was fastened with strong ropes and shipped on the Erricson Line of steamers. The chest was placed on deck, and Mrs. Adams came down to Maryland to accompany it northward, knowing that as a black woman she would also be assigned to the deck. During the night she untied the ropes and opened the lid, and, as William Still wrote in *The Underground Rail Road*, "nerved the heart of poor Lear to endure the trying ordeal of her perilous situation." After a voyage of eighteen hours, the steamer arrived, Mrs. Adams debarked, and the chest was taken off and sent to the home of William Still, where it was opened again for Green to escape. She remained several days with the Stills before going on to Elmira to marry Adams, a runaway who fled at the same time she did and made his way to freedom and marriage.

Helping Lear Green escape may have been Mrs. Adams's only abolitionist activity, but this attempt was dangerous for both women and as emotionally trying for Mrs. Adams as was Green's ordeal in the chest. Mrs. Adams obviously had many reasons for wanting her future daughter-in-law removed from a slave state. Most of these quiet escapes were not written about, but William Still kept extensive notes about those he helped and told their stories in his history of the Underground Railroad. He also kept Lear Green's chest as "a fitting memorial."

Two men named Smith—one black, one white, not related—helped Henry Brown escape slavery from Richmond, Virginia, in 1849. Brown, though a slave, was a skilled worker in a tobacco manufacturing factory. When he married he was given special considerations, and he set up an independent household for his wife, a slave, and his children. The Browns had a better life than most slaves, but his wife's owner had the wife and children sold. Their lives were torn asunder, and the agitated and distraught Brown determined to be free.

Brown turned to James Caesar Anthony Smith, a free black, for help. Both men belonged to a church choir, and Smith had been a conductor on the Underground Railroad since 1826. Brown also knew Samuel A. Smith, a white local merchant, who he suspected might help him. Samuel Smith later revealed that he had been a conductor since 1828 and had helped many slaves escape. Brown told Samuel Smith the story of the sale of his wife and children and admitted that he was thinking of escaping. Brown had $166; he offered half to Smith for his help, and $86 was agreed upon.

Brown and James Caesar Anthony Smith discussed ways Brown might escape but could not decide on the best plan. Brown, a religious man, then appealed for higher help: "I prayed fervently that he who seeth in secret and knew the inmost desires of my heart, would lend me his aid in bursting my fetters asunder, and in restoring me to the possession of these rights, of which men had robbed me; when the idea suddenly flashed across my mind of shutting myself *up in a box*, and getting myself conveyed as dry goods to a free state."

A carpenter made a box "two feet eight inches deep, two feet wide, and three feet long," Brown wrote, and on March 29, 1849, he entered the box, bored some small holes to provide air, and brought along a bladder of water. The boxed Brown was to travel by train and steamer to Philadelphia. Samuel Smith was to accompany the box, keep it "This side up with care," and handle any problems. But for some unexplained reason, Samuel Smith did not make the trip. No doubt he took the eighty-six dollars up front. Did he oversleep, have a sudden illness that sent him to a hospital? Or was he too afraid to make the trip? Or was he a confidence man who never intended to take that hazardous journey? We can only speculate, and Brown was virtually silent on the matter, remarking that "the man who had promised to accompany my box failed to do what he promised; but, to prevent it remaining long at the station after its arrival, he sent a telegraphic message to his friend, and I was only twenty-seven hours in the box, though traveling a distance of three hundred and fifty miles."

The box was tumbled about, seldom "this side up" or handled "with care," but Brown survived and was delivered to abolitionists in Philadelphia. William Still was present at the unboxing. Brown became a hero to abolitionists, took "Box" as his middle name, and became a public figure.

Back in Virginia, Samuel Smith was arrested in October 1849 after he boxed up two more slaves who were soon captured. James Caesar Anthony Smith was also arrested, charged

with introducing the two slaves to Samuel Smith and putting
supplies into the escape boxes they were to use. Richard Newman, editor of the *Narrative of the Life of Henry Box Brown*,
suggests that James Caesar Anthony Smith was found not
guilty because he employed a good lawyer to handle his case.
The attorney obviously knew his worth: he charged Smith nine
hundred dollars for services rendered.

Samuel Smith was convicted. After years of incarceration,
he was released from prison in 1856 and left Virginia for
Philadelphia, arriving on June 21 and staying several days
with the Still family.

According to Smith's story, as reported in the *New York
Tribune*, he lost all his property after his arrest, and he was not
allowed to present witnesses at his trial. In prison he was held
chained in a small cell, in hot weather, for five months, and
was stabbed five times by a "bribed assassin." He asserted that
he did not regret his abolitionist activities to "undo the heavy
burdens and let the oppressed go free." He did not explain
why he had not accompanied Brown to Philadelphia as he had
promised to do.

To his Philadelphia supporters, Smith presented himself as
having been a model prisoner, winning the confidence of the
superintendent. Learning of a plot among prisoners, Smith
saved the life of a warder. His good deeds duly noted, the
prison officials tried but failed to get him a pardon. Perhaps
the reports in the *New York Tribune* about Smith are true, and
certainly abolitionists wanted to believe such stories. Unfortu-
nately, escaping slaves were sometimes betrayed or fleeced of
their money. What we do know is that the abolitionists of
Philadelphia helped Smith. The last paragraph of the *Tribune*
story noted, "Pecuniary aid, to some extent, was rendered him
in this city. . . ."

James Caesar Anthony Smith also claimed to have been a longtime conductor on the Underground Railroad, and Brown remained on good terms with him, at least for a time. After Brown escaped, he raised money and engaged Josiah Wolcott to paint a huge panorama called "The Mirror of Slavery." Brown lectured at the panorama showings in 1850, but after the passage of the Fugitive Slave Law of that year he fled to England, taking with him thousands of feet of the panorama and his friend James Caesar Anthony Smith. Brown was a fugitive, a nonviolent civil disobedient in the North; but he was out of danger in England.

Brown and Smith toured with the panorama for less than a year before they had a falling out, probably over money. Smith charged Box Brown with "drinking, smoking, gambling, swearing," but these charges may well have been exaggerated. Smith was appealing for public support as he began his own solo lecturing venture. Brown, it is true, was something of a showman: he mailed himself in a box from one British city to another. Showmanship aside, his escape from slavery was daring and a brazen act of civil disobedience. He was aided in various ways, by two men, one of whom did not fulfill all his obligations. Perhaps the best thing we can say of James Caesar Anthony Smith is that he successfully played a part in helping Brown escape.

Harriet Jacobs, a North Carolina slave, lived almost seven years of self-isolation hidden in a crawlspace in her grandmother's house before she was able to flee by bribing a sea captain to take her north. She wrote in her novelized autobiography, *Incidents in the Life of a Slave Girl*: "While . . . making a bargain to escape from slavery, the trembling victim is ready to say, 'Take all I have, only don't betray me.'" Although Jacobs was suspicious of the captain, he did not betray her. He told her he was a Southerner and his deceased brother had been a slave trader. "But," he said, "it is a pitiable and degrading business, and I always felt ashamed to acknowledge my brother in connection with it." It appears, though, that the captain had no qualms about charging escaping slaves large fees to help them. The captain was a conductor of sorts, obviously a practitioner of civil disobedience, but ethically challenged.

Conductors such as Levi Coffin, William Still, John Rankin, David Ruggles, and many others certainly did not charge slaves for their help. Just the opposite: escapees often arrived penniless and poorly clothed, and were taken into homes where they were fed and given clothes and a place to sleep until they moved on, usually with a gift of travel money. Wives of conductors and other abolitionist women also took on many duties. They were sympathetic listeners to the stories of the fugitives, consoling them for their losses, as many had left behind parents, wives, children, or other relatives. As counselors they helped orient the fugitives to their circumstances and prepare them for the ordeals that lay ahead. Men and women abolitionists, from their own pockets and from funds raised among other sympathizers, provided warm garments, shoes, and travel expenses for those being sent by train or ship on to Canada. In rural areas, conductors incurred other expenses, for they had to provide transportation on to the next conductor, which meant maintaining horses or renting wagons or buggies.

David Ruggles in New York was often destitute because of all the help he offered to the fugitives. Frederick Douglass stayed with Ruggles for a few days after escaping, waiting for his fiancée to arrive from Baltimore. Frederick and Anna were married by the Reverend J. W. C. Pennington, also an escaped slave; Ruggles must have made all the arrangements. When the young couple left for New Bedford, Ruggles gave Douglass five dollars. Perhaps Ruggles was able to get that sum from the Vigilance Committee; if not, he dug into his own mostly empty pockets.

Coffin and Still were astute businessmen, but their abolitionist activities were a drain on their finances. Reverend Rankin had a large family and was not well paid by his church, but he managed to find whatever money was needed to help escapees. Most individual conductors spent their time and money helping slaves without thought of compensation. Samuel Smith may have been an exception.

In addition to helping slaves escape, abolitionists also worked to improve the lives and rights of blacks in the Northern free states, where there were many racial barriers. Blacks, free or escapees, were routinely sent to Jim Crow train cars. Blacks and whites protested, mostly in nonviolent ways.

David Ruggles, one of the least known of the active black abolitionists, in 1841 was subjected to numerous acts of discrimination. In June of that year he attempted to buy a first-class ticket for the steamer trip between New Bedford, Massachusetts, and the island of Nantucket. The captain refused to provide a ticket and seized all of Ruggles's personal papers.

Such discrimination, even violent manhandling, was nothing new to Ruggles, for he had been an activist for several years. He was a Garrisonian, operating a grocery as well as an abolitionist reading room and bookshop. He was the first black journalist; he established his own press to publish his pamphlets on such topics as abusive behavior toward blacks, by both Southerners and Northerners. One of these charged Southern men with violating the Seventh Commandment and their wives with allowing their husbands to father children with slave women. In 1839 he published the *Slaveholder's Directory*, listing the names of police, lawyers, and others who "lend themselves to kidnapping" escaped slaves. He founded the New York Committee of Vigilance in 1835, which helped hundreds of escaping blacks. His mistreatment by police apparently contributed to the loss of most of his eyesight.

Ruggles was often a contributor to the *Colored American*, published by the abolitionist Samuel Cornish, a black Presbyterian minister. The two men had a falling out after Ruggles wrote an article in 1839 about John Russell, the black hotelkeeper in New York said to be keeping captured slaves in his possession before they were returned South. Ruggles inserted the story, which had not been authenticated, in the paper without Cornish's knowledge. Russell sued and won a judgment of six hundred dollars, nearly bankrupting the paper.

Cornish then attacked Ruggles in the *Colored American* and worked to drive him out of the abolitionist movement in New York. Ruggles was required to account for all the monies expended by the Vigilance Committee, and he was unable to explain an expenditure of four hundred dollars. He was forced out of office and left New York. "In truth," writes Graham Russell Hodges, preparing a biography of Ruggles, "the more conservative Cornish and his many allies had tired of Ruggles' radical methods and sought less confrontational means to fight slavery." Ruggles was an aggressive civil disobedient. He engaged in some of his usual abolitionist activities until 1845, when he established a water-cure hospital. Even then he went on writing articles urging the end of slavery.

Ruggles insisted on his rights on public transportation. A few weeks after being attacked by the boat captain in New Bedford, he entered a train car in that city. When the conductor ordered him to the Jim Crow car, Ruggles refused and was dragged from his seat. He insisted, "While I advocate the principles of equal liberty, it is my duty to practice what I preach, and claim my rights at all times." Unlike many Garrisonians, he believed in seeking justice through the courts; he sued the railroad. Blacks found that judges were often biased against them. The Massachusetts judge who heard Ruggles's case was a shareholder in the line that discriminated against blacks. The judge ruled against Ruggles: railroad officials could seat riders wherever they wished to.

About forty black and white abolitionists, including Douglass and Garrison, took the steamer from New Bedford to Nantucket on August 10, 1841. They booked on the same line on which Ruggles had been assaulted. The blacks were told that they would need to ride on the segregated upper deck. Some passengers refused as a matter of principle and would not take passage. After the abolitionists had a parley with the captain, blacks and whites were allowed to use the upper deck—when the weather was fine, it was the preferred place to be during the trip. Nonabolitionist whites from below also came to the upper deck. In this instance it was the white captain who became the disobedient. Segregation by race on trains and steamers had its ludicrous side, especially in this instance with blacks and their supporters enjoying the best location on the boat.

Some blacks and whites began to boycott trains and steamers, finding other ways to travel. Moreover the protests and demands for equal treatment provoked some people to rethink their positions on segregation and racism. The threat of lawsuits and loss of riders also led transportation companies in New England to contemplate abandoning their rules on segregation. Slowly those companies did change their policies, and on April 20, 1843, the Norfolk County Antislavery Society announced that the Eastern Railroad had removed its "colored car," perhaps the last of the lines in that area to do so. In other Northern areas, though, Jim Crow cars persisted.

In the South, blacks could not safely protest segregation in churches except by refusing to attend such services and instead finding a black church, where black ministers worked under numerous restraints. Nevertheless these ministers were often subversive in their preaching about the deliverance of the children of Israel from Egypt and about God's punishment for those who oppressed his people. These messages were easily understood by the congregations. Even widely sung spirituals had hidden meaning. The swinging low chariot may be promising a trip to freedom in Canada as well as heaven.

In free states, when abolitionists lashed out at the policies of segregation, they often instigated sit-ins and walk-outs. These activities were nonviolent and against church policy, not governmental laws. The disobedients were opposed to church traditions with their strong racist overtones, but they were acting alone and as individuals when they led protests. Carleton Mabee offers many examples, but three will suffice.

A black family in Randolph, Massachusetts, acquired a pew in a white Baptist church. When they arrived for the service, the pew was gone. They sat on the floor. When they next went to church, the flooring around their now-removed pew was gone. They stood during the service. Obviously this black family was courageous in what must have been a hostile environment. Several questions come to mind: Were they initially encouraged by a minister who wished to desegregate the congregation? Did the minister, facing opposition, then refuse to support his new church members? Or was the family light-skinned and not identified as black when they actually acquired the pew? What happened to them? Were they forced to places in the segregated gallery? Did they, in disgust, give up on religion entirely? Or did they find another white church where they were welcome, or a black one? The record is silent.

Baptist churches seemed to have troubles with civil disobedient pew holders. A white woman in Newport, Rhode Island, asked a black girl who was a member of the congregation to sit with her. The woman was reprimanded by church officials, and the church refused to renew her pew lease when it came due. The woman made a public protest. She brought a camp stool to church, placed it by her former pew, and sat there during the services. Reporting on the incident, the *Liberator* speculated: "Jesus could not get into many of his churches if he should come this way now, unless he took the gallery." The *Liberator* did not follow up this story, but it is likely that the white woman who defied the church finally walked out to no church or to a church with a no-segregation policy.

A white minister in Newark, New Jersey, walked to his church with a black woman who was a servant in his home. He seated her in the pew with his wife, and for this defiance of custom he was fired.

Blacks were more likely to walk out than to protest by sitting in, though the latter did occur. Humiliated by segregated seating arrangements and by ministers who offered communion to white parishioners first, blacks began to leave churches where such situations occurred, sometimes individually, sometimes in groups. Free black churches developed rapidly in the decades before the Civil War. The African Episcopal denomination was founded in 1816, and the African Methodist Episcopal Zion denomination in 1821. Black Baptist and Methodist churches experienced the largest growth. By 1861 there were thirteen black churches in New York and nineteen in Philadelphia.

Schooling for black children was forbidden in the South, and in free states black children were often denied admission to white schools and sent to poorly equipped and maintained black schools. Black parents began to use methods of civil disobedience to protest this segregation.

After Frederick Douglass moved to Rochester, New York, in 1847, he enrolled his nine-year-old daughter Rosetta in Miss Tracy's Seward Seminary. He was out of town when Rosetta actually began classes. When he returned home, he asked her about school. As Douglass wrote:

"'I get along pretty well,'" she responded, "with tears in her eyes"; she continued, "'but father, Miss Tracy does not allow me to go into the room with the other scholars because I am colored.'"

An angry Douglass visited the school the next day to confront Miss Tracy. She reported that she had discussed Rosetta's admission with the trustees, and they had raised objections.

Miss Tracy thought of being disobedient, but "then she remembered how much they had done for her in sustaining the institution." Her compromise was to keep Rosetta in a separate (presumably equal) room "for a term or more" and thereby overcome the prejudice against her.

Douglass announced that he and his wife would remove Rosetta from the school. Douglass was by this time a national figure and the editor of the *North Star*, which he published in Rochester. He let Miss Tracy know that the entire country would learn of her "unwomanly conduct." Through his lecturing, his contact with abolitionist newspaper editors, and his own *North Star*, he certainly could do so.

Although Miss Tracy obviously sought to follow the wishes of the trustees, she decided to question her students about allowing Rosetta to sit in the class. She probably assumed that if the trustees were prejudiced, the students would be too.

When Miss Tracy polled the students, one girl said she didn't care if Rosetta stayed. Miss Tracy exposed her own prejudice: "Did you mean to vote so? Are you *accustomed* to black persons?"

Miss Tracy was not receiving the answers she wanted to hear. She then asked the children where Rosetta would sit if she were allowed in the room.

"By me, by me, by me," was the response.

Foiled by her unprejudiced students, Miss Tracy sent a note home to parents that day asking for comments on this racial matter.

One parent, the editor of the *Rochester Courier*, objected to having Rosetta in the school. Upon receiving this single negative response, Miss Tracy expelled the child, sending Rosetta home with her books and pencils. Douglass quickly found another school for his daughter. He did have his say about the prejudiced editor: "We differ in color, it is true, (and not much in that respect,) but who is to decide which color is most pleasing to God, or most honorable among men? But I do not wish to waste words or arguments on one whom I take to be as destitute of honorable feeling, as he has shown himself full of pride and prejudice."

After this mistreatment of Rosetta, Douglass worked actively to desegregate the public schools in Rochester. Because black student enrollment increased, a new black school was soon needed on the east side of the city. But if segregation were ended, a new school would not be needed. The "pro-slavery Irish faction," Douglass said, won the day and a new, segregated school was ordered. To save money, the school board decided not to put up a new building; instead it contracted with

the black Zion Methodist Church to hold classes in the church
basement. The church trustees, Douglass pointed out, "sanctified . . . the spirit of caste, by which we are constantly haunted
and tormented." Douglass led the campaign to change school
policy. He kept his own children out of the public schools;
for part of the time they were tutored by a Quaker teacher.
The Rochester schools were finally desegregated in 1857, and
Douglass then enrolled his children in the public schools.

Boycotts of schools were often effective after months or
years of mass desertions by black children. Depriving black
children of equal educational opportunities obviously preyed
on the minds of some white parents, who then joined black
parents in attempting to open the schools to all. The protest
meetings, largely black, but with some white support, helped
some school boards reach a favorable decision about the
need for desegregated schools. Without doubt, though, black
children suffered during the boycotts, for their education was
interrupted while protests continued against intransigent
school boards.

Some black parents with economic means (there were not
many wealthy blacks, but they did exist) refused to pay taxes
to school districts that were segregated. These were classic
cases of noncooperation in the Thoreau mode. For example,
Robert Purvis, the wealthy black, had an estate at Byberry,
Pennsylvania, and was a major taxpayer in the township. In
1853, finding that the school district had introduced separate
schools for black children, he removed his children from school
and had them privately taught. He then refused to pay school
taxes. Purvis was the second-largest taxpayer in the district.
The school desegregated.

While blacks, sometimes aided by abolitionists and other
sympathetic whites, had some successes in the free states in

desegregating schools, large numbers of schools continued to restrict black children to segregated and inferior conditions.

Many abolitionists and blacks also boycotted goods produced by slaves: sugar and molasses, tobacco, and cotton goods such as sheets, towels, and cloth for making dresses, shirts, and undergarments. Carleton Mabee suggests the main reasons for these boycotts: they "ranged from the unworldly belief that the boycott was primarily a means for abolitionists to purify themselves individually from cooperation with the sin of slavery to the frank avowal that the boycott was the wielding of economic power to compel the owners to free their slaves." Gandhi would later use this tactic in India, urging that English-made cloth not be used and that those seeking independence from the British should take up spinning, as he himself did.

One of the most prominent merchants selling "free" goods was Levi Coffin, who conducted his business in Cincinnati. Coffin traveled to the South to purchase free goods, never making a secret of his aversion to slavery, though willing to engage in conversation with slaveholders he met.

The boycott of slavery-produced goods was largely symbolic, for those who produced these goods were never significantly damaged economically. It might have been different if all the people in free states and in Europe had demanded free-labor goods. They did not.

Nonviolent activists involved in civil disobedience left a record of successes and failures chronicled in the *Liberator* and other papers, and in the journals, autobiographies, and biographies of the participants. They experimented with ways to end racial discrimination. They had strong leaders such as Douglass and Garrison, but they quarreled frequently among themselves, making their work less effective. Douglass broke with Garrison, and Garrisonians then wrote and spoke harshly about Douglass. Douglass did not hide his differences with the Garrisonians. Ruggles was forced out of the abolitionist movement in New York.

Although nonviolent activists did not bring about universal emancipation, in the decades before the Civil War, they did, through the Underground Railroad and various vigilance committees, help thousands of slaves who fled the South. And they were able to force the desegregation of some public transportation lines in free states. They pointed out the fallacy of segregated churches in the North, though in most cases white churches continued their segregated ways. Blacks then began to found their own churches. They also desegregated some school systems in free states.

During the three decades from 1830 to 1861, blacks and whites practicing nonviolent civil disobedience acted individually or in groups to confront racism in the free states and more quietly in slave states, where their activities placed them in great danger. While living at his isolated cabin on Walden Pond, the individualist Thoreau, who opposed the Mexican War that he believed was being fought to extend slave territories, and refused to pay his taxes in support of the war, was arrested and went to jail. His defiance was brief, for someone else, without Thoreau's permission, paid the taxes. Thoreau spent only one night in jail. But from that experience and from his belief that slavery was wrong and that laws supporting slavery should be broken, he wrote his famous and enduring document on civil disobedience.

CHAPTER

III

CIVIL DISOBEDIENCE AND

JIM CROW RAILROAD CARS

"When I first went among the abolitionists
of New England, and began to travel,
I found this prejudice [against color]
very strong and very annoying."
—From Frederick Douglass,
My Bondage and My Freedom

❧ Nonviolent attempts to end segregation on public transportation in the free states were ongoing through the 1840s
and 1850s. To dramatize that struggle, we reprint in this chapter the long letter by John A. Collins about this festering problem. (Explanatory footnotes are added at the bottom of the
page.) The letter was addressed to William Lloyd Garrison and
published in the *Liberator* on October 15, 1841.

Collins (1810–1879) was a graduate of the Andover Theological Seminary, a Garrisonian, and a member of the Nonresistance Society. He was also general agent (director) of the
Massachusetts Anti-Slavery Society. Garrison wrote in the *Liberator* for August 27, 1841, that Collins had "set at work

nearly all the machinery that has kept the cause in motion for the last three years" and that he was a man of "almost superhuman energy."

Collins played a significant role in Douglass's early days in the abolitionist movement. Douglass escaped from slavery in 1838 and settled in New Bedford, Massachusetts, where he did manual labor. He subscribed to Garrison's *Liberator*, and in the summer of 1841 he attended a large anti-slavery convention in Nantucket. He was invited to speak on "the scenes through which I had passed as a slave," and his address "excited" the audience. Collins sought him out that night and urged him to become an agent of the Massachusetts Anti-Slavery Society. After equivocating, Douglass agreed to try the work for three months. A new life opened up for him. His work was successful, and he soon moved his family to Lynn, Massachusetts, a Quaker stronghold. Collins often accompanied Douglass to abolitionist events.

In 1843, Collins left active work in the abolitionist movement to found a utopian community based on socialist principles. Before three years had gone by, the experiment failed, and Collins left the movement.

He was a vivid writer, combative in arguing his principles and at times wryly humorous. Like Garrison, his language could be harsh. Here is his long report:

Dear Garrison:

While our feelings are excited with horror and indignation at the recent outbursts of lynch law and violence upon the poor defenceless colored people of Cincinnati, it becomes my painful duty to chronicle the mobocratic proceedings of the Eastern Rail-Road Corporation for the past few weeks, upon the colored people and their friends, as they have come under

Frederick Douglass escaped from slavery in 1838, settled in Massachusetts, and became a champion of the anti-slavery cause. *(National Portrait Gallery, Smithsonian Institution /Art Resource, NY)*

my own personal observation. Never was there a more malicious and hyena-like spirit exhibited by any body of men than by the servants of this company, who are acting under the orders and command of STEPHEN A. CHASE, the Superintendent,— who, by the way, is an influential member of the Society of Friends of the orthodox school.[1]

---

1. Many Quakers were members of anti-slavery societies and conductors on the Underground Railroad, helping slaves reach freedom, but others were not sympathetic to blacks.

You, no doubt, recollect the affray which took place the
6th of August last, on board the cars, on our way from Salem
to Boston, when a respectable colored woman was invidiously
selected out, insulted, and ordered into the *"negro car,"* notwithstanding a great number expressed their unwillingness to
have her leave. But, after the conduct I learned that she was
not a slave, but bona fide a free woman; nothing but her eject-
ment would satisfy him.[2]

On the 8th of September, a more flagrant outrage was
committed upon the person of our friend Douglass, who happens to be one or two shades darker than Daniel Webster.[3] We
purchased our tickets in Newburyport, for Portsmouth, being
on our way to Dover, N.H. to attend the annual meeting of the
Stafford County Anti-Slavery Society. Douglass took his seat
by my side, in one of the long cars, as there was no difference
in the price of our tickets. No sooner were we seated, than the
conductor made his appearance and peremptorily ordered
Douglass to leave, and to take his seat in the forward car,
meaning the *"Jim Crow,"* though he felt ashamed to call it by
that name. It was in vain for those around him to remonstrate
against the proscriptive policy. It was useless for us to inquire
the reason why he, in particular, should be selected out from
all the rest of the passengers, and particularly when no one
had entered a complaint. I demanded his authority. A placard
was instantly torn down from a conspicuous position it occupied near the door of the car, which gave the conductor, by a
rule of the Directors, the right to seat passengers where it

2. The conductor.
3. Douglass was new to the movement when this letter was written,
and Collins had perhaps not seen the name written out. He used the
spelling "Douglas" throughout. We have silently made the correction.
Daniel Webster had dark skin and was called "Dark Dan."

might please him; and all who purchased tickets must be subject to this rule. I remarked that that rule gave him no authority to order Mr. Douglass out of the car. At this the conductor's ire was fiercely kindled, and his little fist flourished about my head quite gracefully. I was ordered to leave my seat, that he might meet with less obstruction in "snaking" my friend out of the cars. This I refused to do, and coolly remarked, "If you haul him out, it will be over my person, as I do not intend to leave this seat.—That the rule, as he interpreted it, was a violation of the State Constitution, and that, if Mr. Douglass had violated a constitutional rule of the Company, it could be nothing more than trespass, and they had the law of the Commonwealth to appeal to; and that to lay violent hands upon him should be nothing more nor less than lynch law." The recent decision of *Justice* (!) *Crapo*[4] of New Bedford was appealed to as good authority.[5] The conductor left the cars, and returned in a few moments followed by four or five of the Company's minions, with a fiendish smile and a careless indifference expressed in their countenances, appearing like so many bloodhounds, waiting for the orders of their masters to seize him, which were no sooner given than they laid hold of him, like so many hyenas, and snaked him out over me in a tangent and thrust him into the "*negro car*," with a "Go there, that's good enough for you, d--n you"—according to the testimony of Richard Hood, who stood by at the time. Our friend, George Foster, of Andover, to bear his testimony against this prescription against colored people, entered the "negro car," but was ordered out, as he "was not black enough to ride there." I was considerably injured in the affray, and Douglass

4. Collins did not wish readers to miss the scatological name.
5. The judge had ruled against David Ruggles, finding that the line had the authority to assign seating to passengers.

suffered some injury in his clothes. After the train got under-weigh, the conductor returned, greatly incensed against me, and made use of the most insulting language.

One of the conductors entered the "negro car," and to con-sole friend Douglass remarked that "this rule of the Directors can't be so bad, for the *churches*, you know, have their *'negro pews.'* What a commentary on our christianity!"[6]

On Tuesday morning, the 28th ultimo, I purchased at the Boston depot a ticket for Newburyport. When we arrived at Lynn, I descended from the cars, according to previous arrange-ments, to see a lady on board, who was anxious to attend the county meeting at Newburyport. My female friend entered the car, followed by Douglass, and our friend J. N. Buffum[7] who

6. Douglass found out about segregation in Northern churches early in his time in New Bedford. He planned to join the mostly white Elm Street Methodist church, which had about a half-dozen black members who sat in the balcony. Douglass learned during the first service he attended that the color bar was strong there. The Lord's Supper sacrament came after the sermon. All whites were first served with the bread and wine, then the min-ister called out, raising his voice "to an unnatural pitch, and looking to the corner where his black sheep seemed penned, beckoned with his hand, ex-claiming, 'Come forward, colored friends!—come forward! You, too, have an interest in the blood of Christ. God is no respecter of persons. Come forward, and take this holy sacrament to your comfort.' The colored members—poor slavish souls—went forward, as invited. I went out, and have never been in that church since. . . ." Douglass then joined a black church, the Zion Methodist, and served as a local preacher for a time. He left that religious group too when he "found that it consented to the same spirit which held my brethren in chains."

7. A successful Quaker from Lynn, Massachusetts, Buffum was one of several dissidents who later were to leave the Friends to be a more radical reformer. At first Douglass and Buffum were friends. In 1845 they sailed to-gether on the *Cambria* to the British Isles. Douglass was not allowed to take a cabin, and the two men went steerage. In Dublin they stayed with Richard D. Webb, the publisher who was to bring out an edition of Douglass's *Nar-rative*. Webb wrote to Maria Weston Chapman, Secretary of the American Anti-Slavery Society, that Douglass's "offensive and ungrateful behaviour

brought up the rear. Douglass and myself occupied one seat—the lady sat in front of us, and Buffum sat behind. We had scarcely exchanged salutations before our old friend, the conductor, made his appearance, greatly enraged. He is a small, spare and feeble looking man, with nothing malicious in his countenance. Nature had not qualified him with strength, force and resistance sufficient to enable him to perform, with pleasure, the mean business in which he was then engaged. He was pale as death. His lips quavered—his whole frame shook, and his knees, like those of Belshazzar, smote together.[8] From my heart I pitied him. He forced up his courage sufficiently to collar Douglass, and ordered him out.

"Can't I ride with him, if he goes into the forward car?" said Buffum. "I want to have some conversation with him, and I fear I shall not have another opportunity so favorable."

---

to James N. Buffum towards whom he has been absolutely insolent—not only in my house but elsewhere—that first 'battered my esteem for him.'" He continued, "How Buffum has put up with the conduct from one for whom he has done so much, is past my comprehension. . . ." Chapman had apparently charged Buffum to look after the money during this trip, and when Douglass learned that, he felt he was being condescended to and took out his anger on Buffum. Douglass was a prickly man and may have imagined Buffum's condescension.

8. Collins was referring to Daniel 5:1–31. King Belshazzar, his princes, wives, and concubines drank from the golden vessels "taken from the temple of the house of God." Then fingers of a man's moving hand wrote on the wall of the palace, and the king's thoughts were troubled "and his knees smote one against another." Daniel was called to interpret the message on the wall, and he did so:

"God hath numbered thy kingdom, and finished it."
"Thou art weighed in the balances, and art found wanting."
"Thy Kingdom is divided, and given to the Medes and Persians."

The interpretations were correct: Belshazzar was killed that night.

Collins's reference goes far beyond knocking knees to tell his biblically knowledgeable readers that the writing was on the wall and that those who supported slavery were out of favor with God and would be deposed.

"No," quoth the little man in grey. "I'd as soon haul you out of his car, as I'd haul him from this."

"There are but very few in this car," said Douglass very modestly, "and why, since no objection has been made, do you order me out?"

"I've no objection to ride with him—let's take a vote on the question," said one.

"That's just what I want—let us have a vote on the question," replied Buffum.

"I've no objection to that step," cried a third.

Not the least heed, however, was given to this. Duty had to be performed to the satisfaction of the pseudo quaker and superintendent of the corporation, Stephen A. Chase.

I inquired for his authority for ejecting him, but to no purpose.

"If you will give me any good reason why I should leave this car, I'll go willingly; but, without such reason, I do not feel at liberty to leave," said Douglass; "though," he continued, "you can do with me as you please, I shall not resist."

"You have asked that question before," quoth the trembling conductor.

"I mean to continue asking the question over and over again," said my colored friend, "as long as you continue to assault me in this manner."

"Give him the reason," cried one voice after another, in tones too positive to be misunderstood.

The conductor found himself in quite an embarrassed situation. He felt it would not do to force him out without a reason, and yet the reason amounted to no reason at all. He finally made up his mind to say, in a half-suppressed, half-audible voice, "Because you are black." The giving utterance to this thought oppressed him. It stuck in his throat, like Macbeth's *Amen.* He could not speak out boldly, "Because you are black."

By this time, there was quite a gathering around the cars. The little pale man again collared Douglass, but, finding him inflexible in his determination to remain, relinquished his grasp, and began to make preparation for snaking him out. The lady, who sat in front of us, was in his way. "Leave this seat, Miss—it's no place for you—go forward into the ladies' car."

She hesitated, and gave him a look, which expressed in no ambiguous language, "Please let me alone, sir, and go about your own business."

This greatly excited our host, who seized hold of her arm, and very unceremoniously led her to the other end of the car, and called some eight or ten of the Company's minions to his aid.

"Snake out the d---d nigger," cries one.

"Out with him," responded another guardian of the "Peculiar institutions" of the south.

The gang of men stood in a leaping posture, with their hands extended and fingers half bent, ready for the going forth of the command of the captain to seize him.

The word was given—"Take him out!"

Five or six, like so many tigers, laid hold of Douglass, but he happened to be exceedingly heavy, as the laws of gravity were in full force. His attachment to his seat was so great, that these half a dozen bullies found it no easy task to snake him out over me.

"D--n that Collins," cries one of them, "out with him, out with him."

Whereupon five or six laid violent hands upon me. One gave a severe blow upon the back part of my head, and another hit me in my face, cutting my lip considerably. Like my friend Douglass, I did not feel inclined to part with my seat at the command of these ruffians, if I may be allowed the use of such an expression; in consequence of which, our seat gave way, and we, with five or six of these villains hold of our head, arms and legs, were dragged out head foremost, and deposited upon the ground in no very gentle manner. One of the gang gave me a very severe kick in my back, in consequence of which I am lame at the present time. I was so badly bruised that my person, in various parts, is black and blue. Buffum remained behind with Douglass, whose baggage was thrown out after him.[9]

I was allowed to pass on in the same train. Soon after the cars started, the conductor approached me, and made use of the most abusive language. I asked him, if he was employed by the company to insult passengers, and if so, I considered him the most faithful servant I ever met with; and then turned myself around, and began to read. He shook his little fist about my head a few times, and was greatly enraged because I would

9. Douglass's account in *My Bondage and My Freedom* of this and similar incidents on trains is bland in comparison with Collins's account. Douglass wrote that he regarded Jim Crow cars as a custom "fostering the spirit of caste." He made it a rule to seat himself "in the cars for the accommodation of passengers generally." He would refuse the order of the conductor to move, be dragged from the car, "beaten, and severely bruised."

Douglass was, in his actions, declaring civil disobedience. He acted nonviolently, and usually there was no publicity about the incident. What is different in this Lynn incident is a sympathetic observer had the reporting skills to describe the scene of violence against a black man and then publish that account. Collins did not stage the act of civil disobedience, but he knew Douglass, and he knew that Douglass would not readily go into a Jim Crow car. All Collins had to do was travel with Douglass for a few days and he would have an incident to describe in the *Liberator*.

We have reparagraphed the dialogue in this and other sections of the letter.

hold no conversation with him. I was now left to myself until we arrived at Salem.

Soon after our arrival at Salem, the little man came up in quick step, with much satisfaction expressed in his countenance, followed by a large portly man with a straight coat and broad brim (who from the appearance of his face, would be a fine subject for the celebrated John Hawkins to experiment upon) introducing me thus—"This is that fellow."

Whereupon the ruffian quaker[10] said, "Thou must get out of this car; thou can't travel upon this road."

"Can't travel upon this road?" said I. "You will, I presume, give me a reason."

"I want no words from thee," pointing his finger at the door. "Thou quarrels so, the passengers can't ride with thee," quoth the broad brim.

"Yes," cried out a southerner, (in spirit at least,) who had previously declared that he should like to catch the damned abolitionists at the south, and if they didn't get well used up, he was greatly mistaken.

"Ar'n't thee going out?" continued this representative of the peace principles, who was chairman of the committee which recommended that that noble and philanthropic man, Wm. Bassett, should be disowned from the Society.[11]

"If thee don't get out," Chase continued, "I'll call the brakemen to haul thee out;" and suiting his actions to the word, departed in pursuit of his servants to do his dirty work, when another well-dressed, portly being wearing the human

10. Stephen A. Chase, the Quaker involved in this incident, was called by abolitionists the "Bulldog of Prejudice."

11. Bassett was threatened with expulsion from the Quakers because of his outspoken anti-slavery activities conduced outside of Friends circles. The conservatives, led by Chase, won the struggle, and Bassett was expelled.

form, swaggered into the car, with a "Yes, this is not the first time you have made a disturbance on this road; and now walk out, Sir, and that quickly, too."

I afterwards was informed that his name was Neal, the President of the corporation. It was useless for me to hold out my ticket, showing them that my fare had been paid through to Newburyport. Out I must go. Chase now entered with his poor hired tools, ready to drag me out. Seeing that violence was about to be used, and feeling that I had borne a faithful testimony, and being not a little sore from my previous treatment, I took my valise, and left the cars, and had to hire a private conveyance to Newburyport! Thus I had literally fallen among highway robbers.[12]

On Wednesday evening, the 29th ult., I attended a large meeting in Lynn, at which strong resolutions were unanimously passed condemning, in no measured terms, the conduct of the corporation.[13]

Thursday morning, Sept. 30th I proposed to my Lynn friends to go up to Boston, to get an account of these proceedings into the *Liberator* and was accompanied to the depot by my particular friend, Jona. Buffman. While in conversation with him, the Boston and Salem trains both stopped at the Lynn depot. It was not many minutes before I heard a shriek

12. Those using civil disobedience tactics were often abused by bus drivers and other representatives of companies enforcing segregation policies—and by the police.

13. Buffum wrote about the effects the demonstrations were having: "I am convinced that the agitation growing out of these incidents will do much good. In Lynn, it has been the means of bringing new converts to our cause; and even in Salem, where it has seemed as if nothing short of Almighty judgments would wake them from their guilty slumbers, the people are roused into active discussion. Indeed, everywhere I go, I hear men and women talking of these shameful transactions."

from a female in one of the cars and was informed that a woman was being dragged out. I immediately went on board, and took my seat near friend Bossom, of the *Yankee Farmer*.[14] The first part of this affray did not come under my observation. The first thing I observed was three men having this woman by her head and heels, carrying her out of the cars. They laid her down upon the ground in no very gentle manner. Mr. Bosson, and Mr. Valentine of Worcester, saw Shepard, a great two-fisted, profane fellow, and one of the conductors, strike the woman with great force.

It appears that this unfortunate woman was Mrs. Greene, the talented and highly respected Secretary of the Lynn Female Anti-Slavery Society. Her hair is straight and complexion light. Heretofore, she has been permitted to ride in the long cars. This morning, she got into the cars, as usual, with her infant, only five months old. The conductor ordered her out, but she refused, not feeling at liberty to debase herself by voluntarily entering the proscribed Negro car, and particularly after having paid a full price for her ticket. Five ruffians, with abundance of oaths and horrid imprecations, were ordered to carry her out. Mrs. Greene informed me that an attempt was made by one of these blood-hounds to wrench her infant from her arms, but she held on to it, and the consequence was the side of the babe was hurt by the grip of the conductor. Mrs. Greene's husband, learning that his wife and child were being roughly handled, and being moved with the feelings of a parent and husband, rushed to their rescue, but was repulsed from the car, and sent back with a bloody face! By this time, the mother of Mrs. Greene, learning what was going on, ran

14. The *Yankee Farmer* was an agricultural magazine published in Boston.

up to the aid of her daughter, and, though unable to write, left her *mark* upon the face of one of the mobocrats, which will not disappear by a month's washing.[15]

While this affray was being settled between the conductors and the insulted and persecuted colored people, my friend Bosson, whose feelings were greatly excited on account of the injuries the company's servants were inflicting upon the innocent and defenceless colored people, ventured to open a window of the car and remonstrated with them; whereupon one of them poured out upon him a volley of curses, which were frightful to listen to—and threatened, unless he held his tongue, to serve him worse than they had the d--d nigger!

No sooner had we left the station than Shepard, the conductor, entered the car in which we were seated, and with horrid imprecations, anathematized Mr. Bosson in unmeasured terms. He called him a d--d scoundrel and a liar; said he was the cause of all this disturbance, and flourished his great brawny fist around his face; and said that he knew his name was Collins, and he'd be d---d if he could ride on that road. "He'd not have such a cursed skunk on board," or something to that effect;—that he (Collins) would have to leave the cars when the train arrived at the other depot. To save Mr. Bosson from the contents of the conductor's foul mouth, I informed him that my name was Collins; whereupon the anathemas of his delicate tongue were showered in great wrath upon my poor devoted

15. Mrs. Mary Greene was nonviolent during this episode of civil disobedience, but her husband and mother were not. The various abolitionist groups at the time often debated the rights of disobedients to use violence for self-protection.

The injured Mrs. Greene wrote to the railroad stockholders: "I think I have a right, in common with others, to go in any car I choose. When I behave disorderly, it will be time to order me out."

Some accounts of this incident spell her name "Green."

head. His rage increased when he found that I would hold no conversation with him. He appeared to feel that I was an outlaw, a football for any official dignitary to kick, *ad libitum.* When we arrived at the depot of the Lynn hotel, I was ordered out in a style not at all courteous or ceremonious. I asked the cause.

"Not a word, God d--n you—not a word—I'll let you know that I'm captain of this ship. A'nt you going? If not, I'll haul you out. D--n you, I'll see if you don't go."

Whereupon he retired, and, in about a minute returned with five or six salaried tools, who were about to lay violent hands upon me, when one of them exclaimed, "this a'nt him."

"Then let him alone," replied the conductor; and then, turning to me, said—"God d--n you, if you are not him, you may ride." When he went round the cars to gather up the tickets, not having procured one, I offered him a dollar bill. He turned his head from me very cavalierly, and held out his hand, saying "Damn it, give me the change."

I replied that I had no change.

"God d--n you, give me the change."

At this, I was about to pocket my purse, when he turned round upon me with a "Damn you, do you suppose I'm going to carry you to Boston for nothing?"

"Yes," I remarked, "unless you change the bill."

"Well, then, give me the bill."

I took my change, turned myself around, and was compelled to listen to his foul-mouth abuse poured out upon Mr. Bosson till we arrived in East Boston, when we were released.[16]

16. Later in the decade, Thoreau in his essay on civil disobedience wrote of such men as the conductors and brakemen who abused black and white passengers: "The mass of men serve the State thus, not as men mainly, but as machines, with their bodies. They are the standing army,

Having an appointment to address a meeting at Lynn the same evening, I embarked at 6 o'clock for that place. As I was entering one of the long cars, I saw an individual apparently in a great rage, followed by a large number of savage looking fellows, advancing towards the middle of the car, who exclaimed "Take out that d---d nigger—out with him."

"I'm willing to have him remain," said one.

"So am I," said another.

"There is no objection to his riding here," said a third, fourth, fifth, sixth, and so on.

But it was all to no purpose. The petty tyrant had willed it, and it must be done as he had commanded; and the poor colored man disappeared in the twinkling of an eye.

The conductor immediately reappeared with his herd, with wrath burning in his face and oaths and blasphemies rolling from his mouth.

"D--n you," said he to some one who had remonstrated with him. "I can take out any two of you. I'll let you know, God d--n you, that I'm not to be played with. I've plenty of servants at my command, and if you say a word, I'll serve you worse than I did the nigger."

"I'll express my opinions freely," said one, "and I consider this a brutal act."

"I consider this barbarous," said another.

"I should like to have you attempt to haul me out," said a third.

---

and the militia, jailers, constables, posse comitatus, &c. In most cases there is no free exercise whatever of the judgment or of the moral sense, but they put themselves on a level with wood and earth and stones; and wooden men can perhaps be manufactured that will serve the purpose as well. Such command no more respect than men of straw, or a lump of dirt."

The conductors and brakemen in this account by Collins served the railroad corporation just as Thoreau said jailers served the state.

"So should I," said a fourth.

"God d--n you, out with them," said this bully, and a scuffle ensued, and I can't say who or how many of them (but three or four at least) were either hauled, thrust, or pulled out sans ceremonie, and were forbidden to enter the cars again. Report says that they had all paid their passage.

I have been thus particular in giving the narrative of this memorable transaction that the public may see the extent of the spirit of mobocracy, fostered and sustained by a corporation which has received special privileges from the State to promote the public good; and that the good people may see how closely our liberties are bound up with those of the colored people.[17]

From all appearances, it is evident that there is a hired gang about the Company's depot, to carry into effect its rules, let the consequences be what they may.

Three large public meetings have been held by the citizens of Lynn, embracing all classes, from the most enthusiastic abolitionists to their most bitter opponents. At one of these meetings, a committee of four was unanimously appointed to visit the selectmen, to complain against the mobocratic proceedings of the Rail-Road Company, and to urge upon them the importance of stationing the police about the depots to preserve the peace, which was attended to. Another committee was appointed to make a report to the public with respect to the

17. There are certain similarities between the behavior of conductors who kept New England train cars segregated in the early 1840s and the conduct of bus drivers who maintained the decades-long segregation on public transportation in the South. The struggle in the South of the 1950s was brought to intense public attention by Rosa Parks, who refused to move to the back of the bus and was arrested, precipitating the Montgomery, Alabama, boycott that brought Dr. King to national attention. Gandhi in South Africa also found public transportation segregated.

flagrant outrages committed upon the citizens of this Commonwealth by this Corporation. An interesting document may
be expected from this Committee. The first two nights, they
were unanimous in passing strong and spicy resolutions
against the Rail-Road Corporation. At the third meeting,
Gould Brown,—a stockholder and a fellow-committee man
with Stephen A. Chase to disown Wm. Bassett,—made his appearance and took up for the Corporation. He declared that it
derived authority from its charter to make any rule it should
see fit, even to declaring that no man should ride in their cars
who had more than one leg, and that, if found in the cars, the
conductor would have the right to expel him, or saw off one
of his legs. Mr. Brown, after his usual style, bored his audience
with an extremely long speech, with frequent attempts at wit,
rhetoric, and logic; with how much success you can judge for
yourself. All things went on harmoniously till about half-past
9 o'clock, when a vote was taken to reaffirm the resolutions of
the preceding evening, and which were carried, only a few
hands making their appearance against them in the vote. This
greatly enraged the rummies, who thought Mr. Brown had not
been well treated. Evidences that a mob was brewing led our
friends to adjourn the meeting, when much confusion and
noise ensued. The females were much frightened at the pugilis-
tic manifestations of the mobocrats. The good people of Lynn
affirm that most of the disturbers were imported for the occasion, with how much of truth I am unable to say. The mob dispersed soon after the meeting was dissolved.[18]

It was amusing to watch the movements of Chase, the Superintendent, to brow-beat the Lynn people into terms. In con-

18. Use of mobs to disrupt meetings of abolitionists and, later, civil
rights groups was common. Segregationists often charged that outside ag-
itators were causing the trouble in the South.

sequence of the depot being located in the lower part of the town, it is becoming much more populous and prosperous than the other; consequently, the depot is greatly valued by the good people in that part of the town. Accordingly, on Thursday, the depot was closed, and non-intercourse declared! But, instead of its working in the Company's favor, it turned scores against it. Men came to take passage in the cars for Salem or Boston, as formerly, but were disappointed. Accordingly on Saturday morning, the depot was opened and things now go on as formerly. This was a victory the Lynn people were not prepared to gain so soon.

I saw one of the directors, the other day, who acknowledged the rule was bad, but thought some one should prosecute the company. So far as I have been able to learn, this is the opinion of all the directors. Thus this rail-road corporation is like a great bully, knocking down every one within its reach, and then to appear magnanimous, points to the law. But I will say no more this week. I shall have more to say upon this subject hereafter.

Hastily yours for the right,

J. A. COLLINS

Boston, Oct. 4th, 1841.

Much more was reported in the *Liberator* and other papers about the segregation policies of the railroad company. Frederick Douglass in *My Bondage and My Freedom* wrote: "After many battles with the railroad conductors, and being roughly handled in not a few instances, proscription was at last abandoned, and the 'Jim Crow car'—set up for the degradation of colored people—is nowhere found in New England. This result was not brought about without the intervention of the people, and the threatened enactment of a law compelling railroad companies to respect the rights of travelers."

An African American being expelled from a
railway car in Philadelphia. *(Schomburg
Center, New York Public Library)*

The protest that began with Rosa Parks's arrest in December 1955 in Montgomery, Alabama, went on for just over a
year before segregated seating on city buses was abandoned.

These two civil disobedience struggles, waged in the nineteenth and twentieth centuries, were won by the concerted action of the oppressed and their supporters.

CHAPTER

IV

DANGER: "HAVE TOP EYE OPEN"

Beware of "KIDNAPPERS and SLAVE CATCHERS"
—From an April 1851 poster

✿ We turn to accounts of slaves who fled and were captured, the abolitionists and well-wishers who helped or tried
to help them, and the owners, politicians, police, and courts
that were intent on keeping them slaves. All of these stories
contain acts of civil disobedience; some are nonviolent, but
others took place in the midst of violence.

"SUKEY"

The Reverend John Cross was trained for the Congregational
ministry at the Oneida Institute and held pastorates in his
home state of New York before moving west. He began his
anti-slavery activities before settling in Knox County, Illinois,
where he continued to campaign against slavery. He was not
afraid for his fellow citizens to know of his abolitionist beliefs.
When he published articles and letters in the *Western Citizen*,
the Chicago abolitionist newspaper established by followers of

Benjamin Lundy, he used strong language to castigate his opponents. A thrower of verbal thunderbolts, he used humor and satire in his efforts to help slaves.

Cross was one of several major figures in the Illinois story of Susan (in slavery known as "Sukey") Richardson, her three children, and a young woman named Hannah. These five slaves, called indentured servants in the free state of Illinois, belonged to Andrew Borders of Randolph County in the southern part of the state. Borders, a wealthy, contentious man, was often involved in legal wranglings and was known to be a cruel master to his slaves.

There were only a few abolitionists in southern Illinois where vestiges of slavery still persisted well into the nineteenth century. Many of these opponents to slavery were members of a sect of Presbyterians called Covenanters. They refused allegiance to all state and federal governments, as Carol Pirtle writes in her book on the Underground Railroad in Illinois, because their constitutions failed "to recognize Jesus as head of the State." They would not vote, serve on juries, or hold elective office. They began to oppose slavery as early as 1800.

One of the Randolph County Covenanters, William Hayes, lived on a farm near the village of Eden. He had moved west from Galway, Saratoga County, New York, finally settling in Illinois in 1833. Hayes was not particularly successful as a land speculator, but he knew the northern part of the state from his land dealings and because he had relatives there.

On the night of August 31, 1842, Sukey, her three sons, and Hannah ran away from Andrew Borders and came to the home of Hayes, most certainly a conductor on the Underground Railroad. Usually a conductor would take the fugitives a few miles away to another conductor, or in a free state put the blacks on a boat, train, or stagecoach to Canada. Hayes chose, according to Pirtle, to accompany the runaways northward. It may be that he felt they could not make the journey alone. It is also possible that since he had friends and relatives in the northern part of the state, he felt he could get additional help there for the fugitives.

Hayes probably took the slaves to Chester Landing on the Mississippi River, where they took a steamboat ninety miles upstream to St. Louis and then changed to a packet plying the Illinois River.

On September 5, arriving in an open wagon—which suggests that there were no signs of danger—the slaves were left at the Knox County farm home of John Cross, who was away at the time. Hayes and Cross were probably acquainted. Mrs. Cross was at home with three small children. Hayes must have believed it was safe to leave the escapees with the Crosses.

Jacob Knightlinger, a Knox County justice of the peace, lived near the Crosses and discovered that the five fugitives were there. He put together a band of eight or ten armed men, rode to the Cross home, seized the five blacks, and took them to the jail in Knoxville, Illinois.

That night, as Cross was returning home in a wagon, accompanied by George F. H. Wilson, the two men were stopped about half a mile from Cross's home by Knightlinger, accompanied by eight or ten men on horses. The "gang," as Cross called them, were shouting and spooked the horses, and they bolted. The Knightlinger posse raced in pursuit of the Cross wagon, "howling at each leap of their horses like so many prairie wolves."

At the home of David McLaughlin the horses were stopped by men who used "rails or stakes" to hit the horses over the head. McLaughlin shot at Cross, but his gun misfired. Cross did not return fire; he seems to have been nonviolent throughout the episode. Knightlinger rode up, crying, "Hand them out! Damn them! I'll shoot them!" Knightlinger's threat appears to have been mostly bluster. The wagon was searched, nothing was found, and Cross and his friend were allowed to continue. When Cross reached his house, he learned that the five blacks had been captured.

An angry Cross wrote the *Western Citizen* that Knightlinger and his "ruffian gang" with "rifles, oaths and threats in terrorem performed the chivalrous and DARING EXPLOIT of capturing two negro women and three children; and conducting them in triumph to the jail. . . ." He continued, satirically, "If deeds of she-valory are to be awarded under Captain [President John] Tyler's administration, Knightlinger should be made a brevet Major and Secretary [of Navy Abel Parker] Upshur [a strong supporter of slavery] in his zeal for the 'patriarchal institution,' should present him a wench's petticoat for a banner. . . ."

George Wilson then approached Nehemiah West, another justice of the peace in the county and a friend of William Hayes, to complain about Knightlinger and McLaughlin's violent actions in the affray. The two men were charged, tried, and fined a hundred dollars and court costs. The two then appealed the verdict to the circuit court, and Cross wrote in the *Western Citizen* that residents of the county "will learn whether a jury can be found in Knox County, who will justify such midnight assaults upon the peaceful traveler. If so, all legal protection is gone, and there is no alternative left us under God, but obedience to the prime law of nature to PROTECT OURSELVES." He would use protective violence if the courts failed him, suggesting that he did own a gun. When the matter was heard on appeal, Cross testified, and the case was quashed.

Meanwhile, Borders was intent on gaining the return of his "property," though he admitted that Hannah had served her indenture and was therefore free. Hannah then brought suit in the Knox County circuit court against Borders over the improper time she had served in indentured service. Borders, an unethical, influential man, won that case and then filed suit against those who helped the escapees. He won his case in several ways. According to the *Western Citizen*, he came to the courthouse with a cask of peach brandy "for his old friend the Sheriff," the jury and the lawyers also enjoying the drink. The newspaper reported, "Care had evidently been taken in selecting the jurymen. . . ."

In other action, Borders had the three children seized and reenslaved. Susan remained free, but she never again saw her children. Borders sued Hayes in Randolph County on February 8, 1843, for the then huge sum of $2,500 for his assisting the five fugitive blacks. After a change of venue to Pickneyville, various witnesses presented circumstantial evidence that Hayes had helped the runaways.

Hayes had pleaded innocence, but his friend, Justice of the Peace Nehemiah West, gave a deposition which implicated him. Carol Pirtle explains that West "had been instrumental in the abolitionists' activities to help the five fugitives, and, as such, he no doubt felt that he, like William Hayes, was doing God's work and obeying God's laws." West was a devout man who took his religion seriously. He would not commit perjury; he would tell the truth.

Hayes was found guilty and fined three hundred dollars. However much he might be admired for helping Sukey, Hannah, and the three children, the evidence certainly suggests that Hayes was less than truthful when he pleaded innocent to the charges. He was apparently a nonviolent law violator when he acted as Underground Railroad conductor for the five blacks, thus violating the Fugitive Slave Act. A classic civil disobedient would have admitted his guilt, pled the "higher law" justification, and accepted his punishment.

Borders was not finished with his lawsuits. In November 1843 he brought charges against John Cross, Nehemiah West, and two others for giving sanctuary to his five slaves. All the cases were dropped except for the one against Cross. It was finally heard in the summer of 1844, but Borders did not appear to testify. The prosecution then suggested a continuation until the next term. Cross refused and admitted his guilt. The prosecutor was not prepared to continue, and the case was dismissed. Cross clearly wanted his chance to confront the jury with the moral and ethical issues of slavery. He would have made a stirring defense of his actions, drawing public attention to the issue of slaves in Illinois. Cross was obviously willing to suffer the consequences of his guilty plea; a heavy fine or a jail sentence would have resulted in even more publicity. Unlike Hayes, Cross in this instance was a classic civil disobedient in the mold of Thoreau.

SHADRACH

Shadrach Minkins, known as Sherwood Minkins when he was young (perhaps Sherwood was his birth name), was born a slave in Norfolk, Virginia, year unknown but probably between 1814 and 1822. From Gary Collison's careful research, we know that the young slave was sold several times and that he worked at the Eagle Tavern and at the Hutchings store, whose main business was the sale of liquor. In July 1849 he was sold under the name Shadrach to a commission agent, who then found a buyer for him in November. Shadrach's new master was John DeBree, purser of the Gosport Navy Yard, a

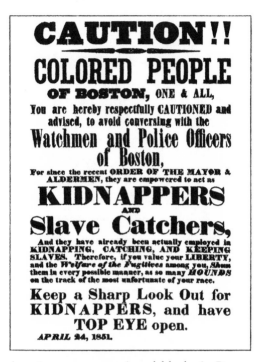

An 1851 poster cautioned blacks in Boston
to beware of dangers under the new Fugitive
Slave Law.

prosperous man with eight whites in his house and six black
slaves and one free black as house servants.

Did Shadrach change his own name, or was it given to him
by an owner before DeBree? The record is silent. The name is
a reference to the story of Shadrach, Meshach, and Abednego
in the book of Daniel in the Old Testament. When the three
men with evocative and poetic names refuse to worship King
Nebuchadnezzar's golden image, the king has them thrown
into the fiery furnace. The three cling to their faith, and the
fire has "no power" over their bodies. Nebuchadnezzar then
speaks: "Blessed be the God of Shadrach, Meshach, and
Abednego, who has sent his angel, and delivered his servants

that trusted in him, and have changed the king's work, and yielded their bodies, that they might not serve nor worship any god, except their own God." If Shadrach Minkins, a religious man, changed his name himself, he may have been thinking of escaping the fiery furnace of slavery.

Shadrach perhaps escaped from DeBree by ship, either by bribing the captain or a crew member for passage or by stowing away. By May 1850 he was in Boston and soon found a job as a waiter at the Cornhill Coffee House, located in the center of the city, about a block from the courthouse.

Shadrach was in Boston at a time of great national tension between North and South over the questions posed by slavery. Should Western territories be admitted to the Union as free or slave states? In light of dissension over slavery, should disunion be considered? Should runaway slaves be allowed to remain free in Northern states? Congress was considering many of these issues.

Three senior senators—Henry Clay of Kentucky, John C. Calhoun of South Carolina, and Daniel Webster of Massachusetts— were major figures who supported the Compromise of 1850, which brought California into the union as a free state; allowed New Mexico and Utah to be organized without determining their status until they were ready to be admitted to the union; prohibited the slave trade in Washington, D.C.; and—most onerous to opponents of slavery—provided a strong law calling for the return of runaway slaves to their masters.

Webster personally disliked the institution of slavery, but he was a constitutionalist, and the Constitution allowed slavery. He was also a driven man seeking the power and prestige of the presidency of the United States and willing to make compromises to gain that end.

The slavery question had festered during the Mexican War. Abolitionists, Whigs opposed to slavery, and others charged that the war was being fought to bring more slave territories into the Union. Anti-slavery forces had rallied around the Wilmot Proviso (1846), which proposed that territories acquired during the Mexican War should not be open to slavery. The proviso was bitterly opposed in 1846 and passed only in the House. In 1847 it was reintroduced, passed in the House, and rejected by the Senate. The Wilmot Proviso helped crystallize the sectional conflict which seemed to many to be incapable of solution. It was a constant irritant to both pro- and anti-slavery forces, who continued to cite it in oratory and in political writings. The issue became even more heated in 1849 when California, part of the Mexican War settlement, sought admission to the Union as a free state.

Although there was much opposition to the Compromise of 1850 in his home state and in other Northern states, Webster fought for it. When President Zachary Taylor died on July 9, 1850, Millard Fillmore, a strong supporter of the Compromise, became president. Webster left the Senate to become secretary of state, and continued to work tirelessly for passage of the various parts of the Compromise. Attacks on Webster grew in intensity. The Quaker poet John Greenleaf Whittier in "Ichabod!" wrote stinging criticism. The poet began:

> So fallen! So lost! the light withdrawn
> > Which once he wore!
> The glory from his gray hairs gone
> > Forevermore!

The poem ended:

> Then, pay the reverence of old days
> > To his dead fame;
> Walk backward, with averted gaze
> > And hide the shame!

Daniel Webster, senator from Massachusetts,
disliked slavery but supported the Constitution that allowed it. *(Library of Congress)*

The reference to the name Ichabod is to I Samuel 4:21:
"And she named the child Ichabod, saying, The glory is departed from Israel. . . ." Whittier makes it clear in the poem
that Webster's reputation has been severely damaged by his
support of the Compromise of 1850. Webster's glory was gone.

The reference to shame in the last two lines is from Genesis 9:20–25. A drunken, nude Noah was covered by his two
sons who walked backward, with a garment over their shoulders, into the tent to cover him, "and they saw not their father's nakedness." Whittier probably used this reference to
Noah's drunkenness because Webster was reputed to be a

heavy drinker. Whittier was also clearly suggesting the shared shame of Noah and Webster.

Shadrach Minkins's work as a waiter in a popular coffee shop placed him in danger because he was not hidden from sight; he was serving food in the heart of Boston. He was seen and recognized by at least one Southerner. His danger was great after President Fillmore signed the new Fugitive Slave Law in September 1850. Many fearful slaves fled to Canada. Within ten days after Fillmore signed the bill, James Hamlet, a fugitive living in New York City, was seized. Within hours he was on his way back to slavery in Baltimore.

Less than a month later, concerned citizens called for a large meeting in Boston's Faneuil Hall to discuss this new menace facing fugitive slaves. Black and white abolitionists and their sympathizers crowded into the hall. Caroline Dall wrote "There was but one feeling among the 6,000 persons assembled there, and that was to trample the law under foot." Frederick Douglass, now rejecting the nonresistance beliefs of William Lloyd Garrison, spoke and recommended that the way to trample the Fugitive Slave Law was to have "a half dozen or more dead kidnappers."

A Vigilance Committee was already in place in Boston to protect fugitive slaves, provide them with legal help, offer funds for escape, and supply information about bounty hunters (called "kidnappers" in many of the posters put up by abolitionists in Boston) who were searching for runaways. Now there was dissension in the committee over the use of violence, as many of the committee members were followers of the Nonresistance Society.

The first major incident concerning fugitives in Boston after the signing of the new Fugitive Slave Law took place without injury or death, but violence was narrowly avoided. On October

19, 1850, Willis Hughes and John Knight of Macon, Georgia, arrived in Boston seeking the return of William and Ellen Craft, who had made a daring escape from slavery. The young Ellen, nearly white, had dressed as an ill male Georgia planter seeking medical care in the North; she was accompanied by dark-complexioned William, posing as the faithful servant. After their escape, the Crafts had become productive citizens of Boston, he as a furniture maker and she as a seamstress.

The Georgia kidnappers immediately faced major problems, for while the federal officials they appealed to said they accepted the Fugitive Slave Law, they did not want their names attached to the seizure of such worthy people as the Crafts. The Georgians finally secured a warrant for the arrest of the black man and his wife, but the Vigilance Committee had a plan to protect the Crafts. The Georgians were identified and described in handbills given wide distribution. The men soon faced mobs and were arrested multiple times for breaking local laws. The Vigilance Committee also had an additional legal plan to help the runaways: because the charges against fugitive slaves were civil, not criminal, the federal marshals could not forcibly batter down the door of the accused. Ellen was sent into hiding, and William chose to defend himself. He barricaded himself in his shop and was heavily armed. A standoff resulted, but no violence. William soon slipped away to a safe house, where he was reportedly guarded by armed black men. The two kidnappers were warned that it was not safe for them to remain in Boston, and they departed the city. Violence was averted, but the Crafts were still in danger, and they left for England.

After the Crafts incident, one abolitionist wrote that Webster had been "whipped" because the Fugitive Slave Law of 1850 had been subverted. Webster was furious at the federal officials who had not done their duty. Those officials were quasi–civil disobedients, not enforcing the law yet not really suffering the consequences of their inaction.

The nonviolent rescue of Shadrach Minkins began in Boston on February 12, 1851, with the arrival of John Caphart (or Capehart), bearing legal papers from John DeBree seeking the arrest and return to Norfolk, Virginia, of his escaped slave. Caphart owned a private jail for the housing of slaves; he was both a slave trader and a slave catcher. His description on a poster prepared by abolitionists was decidedly unpleasant: he was said to be six feet tall, lanky with *"reddish* or *dirty brown"* hair, with "an uncommonly *hard, bad face,* and *ugly,* not only in form and feature, but expression—*a face which seems made for a slave hunter,* or by his business."

Caphart worked quietly behind the scenes and secured a warrant for Shadrach's arrest. In DeBree's papers, Shadrach was described as being twenty-five or twenty-six, about five feet seven inches tall, and with "a complexion between that of a black and a mulatto, which is sometimes called a bacon color, stout, square built, and of pleasing address."

On February 15, at the coffee shop where Shadrach worked, two marshals arrested the fugitive at about 11:30 that morning. He did not resist but was badly frightened. He was taken immediately to the nearby courthouse. The Vigilance Committee had heard no rumors of the attempt to capture him, but word spread rapidly. Committee members and blacks who lived nearby crowded into the courtroom where the hearing was to take place.

The deputy federal marshal, Patrick Riley, was concerned that there might be an attempt to rescue the prisoner that day. The scene was indeed chaotic. About six attorneys—including one black—who worked for the Vigilance Committee were making plans amidst the hubbub for Shadrach's defense. The commissioner hearing the case, George Ticknor Curtis, a strong supporter of the new Fugitive Slave Act, agreed to a postponement for three days. Shadrach's prospects appeared bleak, for DeBree's legal papers were in order, and the prisoner had been identified as the fugitive listed in the documents. The commissioner ordered the courtroom cleared. The blacks in the room were angry and were "looking daggers." Riley had only a few officers with him and was apprehensive as the onlookers walked out slowly. Tensions were high, and provocative words were spoken. In a discussion of what to do if there were an attempt to rescue Shadrach, one of Riley's men said, "Kill the negro."

Eventually the courtroom was cleared except for Shadrach, his lawyers planning his defense, and the marshals and guards. The door was closed and secured. The hall outside was filled with men, some because of other court cases in progress in adjoining rooms, but mostly with angry blacks considering ways to rescue Shadrach. One said, "I'll lose or spill the last drop of blood I have before he shall be carried out of the courthouse."

The published reports of what happened next are confused and somewhat contradictory, but soon after the room was cleared, a signal may have been given. Lewis Hayden, a black who had escaped from Kentucky and was a clothing merchant in Boston, led the charge on the door. Officers inside the courtroom tried to keep the door closed but failed. As many as twenty black men charged into the room. One guard at the door reported that he received blows and kicks, but he was not injured. He did hear one of the blacks say, "Knife him," but another responded, "No, hurt no one."

In the next few minutes there were no injuries as the blacks created disorder and took over the room, no doubt making noise to intimidate the officers. Shadrach, scared and confused, not knowing what was happening, was seized "by the collar and feet" by his rescuers and roughly carried out to the street, losing his hat and coat in the crowded square where blacks were cheering and shouting.

The rescuers, followed by Shadrach's supporters, ran from the square. The guards, if they pursued the prisoner at all, stopped after a few blocks. Lewis Hayden arranged for Shadrach to be taken to the attic in the home of a widow who lived near Hayden's own home, which was certain to be watched. For the moment, Shadrach was safe.

Shadrach's rescue was unusual for the speed with which it was accomplished and because all his rescuers were black. Although at least one of the blacks had a knife and others no doubt had canes or sticks, there was no violence except for the reported kicks and blows directed at the guard. In the words of Carleton Mabee, "noninjurious force" was used—not quite classic nonviolent action, but close.

After a short time, Shadrach was sent on the Underground Railroad to Montreal, with a first stop in Concord, where he was taken to the home of Francis Edwin Bigelow, blacksmith, and his wife, Ann, a leader among the local abolitionists who included the Thoreau family. Lewis Hayden accompanied Shadrach to Concord in a carriage with mismatched horses, indicating that the departure had been hurried. They arrived at the Bigelow home at three in the morning on February 16, 1851. Ann Bigelow prepared breakfast for the anxious and sleepy Shadrach. After he had eaten, Francis Bigelow drove him to an Underground Railroad station in Leominster. From there he was taken to Fitchburg and given a ticket on the train to Canada. When Hayden returned to Boston he was arrested— along with several others—for rescuing the fugitive. Daniel

Webster took an active part in the proceedings, urging prosecution and conviction of the defendants, but to no avail. Hayden's trial resulted in a hung jury; the other defendants were
all found not guilty, or the juries were unable to reach a unanimous verdict.

Thoreau apparently learned immediately of Shadrach's
stop in Concord. He wrote an enigmatic entry in his journal
on February 16, speculating on freedom, slavery, and politicians: "Do we call this the land of the free? . . . We are a nation of politicians—concerned about the outsides of freedom,
the means and outmost defenses of freedom."

Shadrach settled in Montreal, where he became the owner
of a restaurant and then worked as a barber. He married, had
children, and lived the quiet life of a free man. He never returned to the United States. He died in 1875 and was buried
in the Protestant cemetery.

Shadrach the fugitive found himself in a fiery furnace during the time the United States government was attempting to
return him to slavery. Divine intervention did not save him;
mostly nonviolent blacks in Boston did.

THOMAS SIMS

On February 21, 1851, Thomas Sims, a twenty-three-year-old
enslaved mulatto in Georgia, stowed away on a ship bound for
Boston. Once there he contacted his free wife to ask for
money, but his message, which included his Boston address,
was intercepted, and he was arrested on April 3. He was to appear for a hearing before Commissioner George Ticknor Curtis, who had previously been assigned to Shadrach Minkins's
case. The Boston Vigilance Committee met to plan strategy to
save Sims, but its members were deeply divided. Should he be

After a failed attempt to rescue him in Boston, Thomas Sims was returned to slavery in Georgia.

rescued nonviolently, or should force be used? The committee did not make adequate plans, but it did recognize that it needed public support. The local government was hostile and refused the committee's application for a public meeting in Faneuil Hall. The legislature then turned down the request for a meeting on the lawn of the State House. Finally a meeting was held on the Boston Common, followed by one at the Tremont Temple. At both meetings the rhetoric was strong, but no concrete plans to rescue Sims were made.

A nonviolent plan to rescue the fugitive was eventually developed by Thomas Wentworth Higginson, a white Unitarian minister and leading abolitionist; Lewis Hayden, the black merchant who had helped engineer Shadrach's rescue; and the

Reverend Leonard Andrew Grimes, a free black who was pastor of the Twelfth Baptist Church where many escaped slaves worshiped. Mattresses were to be placed underneath the third-floor window of the room where Sims was being held, and Sims was to jump to freedom. Reverend Grimes presented the plan to the prisoner, who agreed to it. The next day, mattresses in place, the plot was foiled. Iron bars were secured over the window of Sims's room. Perhaps the escape plans had been leaked; perhaps the authorities were just being cautious in installing window bars. Apparently the police and marshals believed that a rescue attempt was a possibility, for a large number of men were called in to guard Sims. There were reports of a pack of bloodhounds at the ready. Bloodhounds in the South were routinely used to track escaped slaves, but their use in a free state to pursue fugitive blacks was not common.

The rescue of Sims now appeared impossible. Higginson made a damning analysis: in Boston there was "neither organization, resolution, plan nor popular sentiment" to rescue fugitive slaves. Abolitionists such as Higginson frequently used inflated language, but in this instance there was considerable truth to his charge.

Secretary of State Daniel Webster came to Boston to ensure that the terms of the new Fugitive Slave Law would be carried out. He wrote President Fillmore on April 9 that Sims was safe and predicted that the prisoner would be returned to Georgia.

Sims was brought before the commissioner, who ordered the prisoner returned to slavery. On April 13, Sims was marched to the wharf and placed aboard a ship to Savannah. That day Webster wrote the president that Bostonians had "behaved well" during Sims's deportation, except for some "insane" supporters of the abolition movement.

Six days after leaving Boston, Sims was again in Georgia where he received a public whipping that was almost fatal. Three days later, Webster spoke in Boston, declaring that "a long and violent convulsion of the elements has just passed away, and the heavens, the skies smile again upon us. . . . Let me congratulate you and ask you to congratulate me, that the events of the last year or two have placed us under better auspices; we see clearer and breathe freer. . . . Every citizen feels that he is a man."

Abolitionists were convinced that Webster, whom they regarded as a fallen angel, would now go to any lengths to appease Southern slaveholders in order to further his political aspirations. He would, they believed, willingly sacrifice Shadrach or Sims or any escaped slave captured in a free state. Webster continued to assert that those who attempted to free fugitives were guilty of treason. Several white men and black men, including Hayden, were indicted for their involvement in the Sims case—subject to fines of up to $1,000 and imprisonment up to six months. The trials were slow to be scheduled; eventually they all resulted in hung juries or outright acquittals. Some of those charged were tried twice, but to no avail. Five unresolved cases carried over to the 1853 term were dropped.

The nonviolent attempt to rescue Sims was doomed to failure. He was too well guarded, and the abolitionists failed to develop a workable plan. Sims was again enslaved, but Webster and the federal government failed to convict the civil disobedients who attempted to help him.

After Sims was returned to his master and severely whipped, he was sold and taken to Tennessee. He escaped during the Civil War and returned to Boston. He later worked as a messenger in the Department of Justice and then as a bricklayer in Washington, D.C.

HENRY WILLIAMS

Large numbers of runaway slaves living in Boston fled to Canada after the passage of the Compromise of 1850. Some, including Henry Williams, took their chances and stayed. Williams had escaped from Stafford County, Virginia, in October 1850. According to Henry Thoreau, Williams worked in the same Boston coffee shop where Shadrach, also from Stafford County, had been employed. Perhaps the two had known each other in Virginia. Williams was identified as a fugitive, and warrants for his arrest were quietly issued. The Vigilance Committee was unaware of his plight. When police went to his residence to arrest him on September 30, 1851, Williams was not at home. Learning of his danger, probably from his neighbors, he had made a quick decision to leave. The police did not watch his house, and he fled on foot to Concord, bringing with him to the Thoreaus letters of introduction from William Lloyd Garrison and the Reverend Joseph Lovejoy of Cambridge, brother of Elijah P. Lovejoy, the abolitionist newspaper publisher who had been murdered in Illinois in 1837. Such letters were useful to conductors such as the Thoreaus, for they proved the slave was not a plant sent out by federal officials to interfere in the operation of the Underground Railroad. Of course these letters were also a major threat to Williams and the Thoreaus if they fell into the wrong hands.

The Thoreaus took Henry Williams in for the night, and they obviously talked to him at some length, for Henry Thoreau learned that Henry Williams was an assumed name. Fugitive slaves often took new names to protect themselves. The next day the Thoreaus collected money to help Williams get to Canada; the actual collecting was probably done by the outgoing Mrs. Thoreau, Henry's mother. Henry took Williams to the Concord train station to buy him a ticket to Burlington, Vermont, but Thoreau saw a stranger acting suspiciously, perhaps an indication that he was a Boston policeman trailing Williams. Thoreau and Williams left the station but returned at 5 p.m. to find no lurking policemen, so Thoreau felt it was safe for Williams to leave. Thoreau was certainly not armed; he was breaking the law in a civil disobedient fashion.

Escaped slaves were grateful for the help they received during their flights. William Still in *The Underground Rail Road* published several letters from escaped slaves thanking him and Mrs. Still for efforts in their behalf. When Levi Coffin and his wife were visiting fugitive slaves who had settled in Canada, many of them expressed their gratitude to the couple. Mrs. Still, Mrs. Coffin, and Mrs. Thoreau were among many abolitionist women who helped feed and clothe escapees.

After Williams reached Canada, six hundred dollars was collected to purchase his freedom, and he returned to Boston. Back in Boston he showed his gratitude by purchasing a figurine of Harriet Beecher Stowe's Uncle Tom and Eva and walking out to Concord to give it to Thoreau.

Tensions between North and South continued to heighten over the slavery issue in the 1850s. They were inflamed in 1854 when Senator Stephen A. Douglas of Illinois introduced the Kansas-Nebraska Act. The bill abrogated the section of the Missouri Compromise of 1820 that banned slavery north of 36° 30' latitude. Kansas and Nebraska were to be organized as territories, and the slavery issue was to be decided by the territorial legislatures. Kansas became a bloody battleground. John Brown and his sons killed six pro-slavery men at Pottowattamie and began planning a larger scheme to provoke an uprising of slaves by seizing federal installations at Harpers Ferry, Virginia (now West Virginia). Violence was met with violence as pro-slavery forces retaliated. The North and South moved toward a confrontation.

JERRY HENRY

With the passage of the Fugitive Slave Law of 1850, the wealthy Gerrit Smith, a supporter of the Liberty party and friend of Frederick Douglass, joined by Samuel J. May, minister and longtime anti-slavery agitator, and two other well-known ministers who had escaped slavery—Samuel Ringgold Ward and Jermain W. Loguen—and several others met on October 4, 1850, in Syracuse, New York, to form a Vigilance Committee. They aimed to protect runaway slaves who would, if captured, be subject to return to their masters in the South.

Members of the Syracuse Vigilance Committee were visionaries; they immediately began to make plans to save as many escapees as possible. These abolitionists knew that they had an adamant enemy in the powerful figure of Daniel Webster. In a speech on May 26, 1851, Webster rejected the "higher law" attack on the new Fugitive Slave Law, then being put forward in Massachusetts and New York: "We hear of persons assembling in Massachusetts and New York who set up themselves over the Constitution—above the law—and above the decisions of the highest tribunals—and who say that this law shall not be carried into effect. . . . And have they not pledged their lives, their fortunes and their sacred honor to defeat its execution? . . . For what! For the violation of the law—for the committal of treason to the country—for it is treason and nothing else."

A test case was soon to come. The anti-slavery Liberty party, founded in 1840, met in Syracuse in October 1851. The party rejected Garrison's belief that the Constitution was evil; instead it believed in using political means to deal with the slavery issue. But it could not countenance the return of runaway slaves.

Webster, in a May 26, 1851, speech in Syracuse, had threatened that the Fugitive Slave Law "will be executed in all the great cities, here in Syracuse—in the midst of the next antislavery convention, if the occasion shall arise."

The occasion did arise on October 1 that year, though abolitionists were never able to prove that Webster's threat precipitated the events. The Liberty party convention called by Gerrit Smith and Reverend Samuel J. May was in session when William (Jerry) Henry, a runaway mulatto from Hannibal, Missouri, working in Syracuse as a cooper (a maker and repairer of casks and barrels), was arrested and brought to the local police station. Smith was speaking at the East Genesee Street Congregational Church when the alarm was sounded that Jerry had been arrested. Within minutes, more abolitionist activists crowded into the sanctuary. As Webster had predicted, they pledged their lives, fortunes, and sacred honor to rescue Jerry.

The hearing to identify Jerry as a runaway and to mandate his return to Hannibal was set for an hour after his capture, no doubt in the hope that federal officials could send him on his way back to slavery before the Vigilance Committee could take action.

The activists in the church quickly planned a nonviolent act of civil disobedience. A large crowd rushed to the police office, crowded into the room, and in the confusion and noise managed to set Jerry free. There was, however, a flaw in the plan: a carriage was not at the door to help Jerry make a fast getaway. Instead, Jerry ran and was followed by deputies and volunteers who captured him and returned him to the police office.

But the Vigilance Committee did not give up, and they met to make additional plans for a rescue. This time the abolitionist crowd would storm the jail, take Jerry, put him in a buggy, and spirit him away. Again, the action was to be nonviolent. Reverend Samuel J. May remembered, "Strict injunctions were given and it was agreed not intentionally to injure the policemen. . . . And the last thing I said as we were coming away was, 'If any one is injured in this fray, I hope it may be one of our own party.'"

Jerry was neither composed nor quiescent during his hours of capture. Reportedly he was "yelling like a mad man" and swearing that he "would tear out his master's guts if he could lay his hands on him."

The abolitionist attack on the police station began at 8:30 that evening. The streetlight near the station was extinguished, leaving the area in darkness. Men armed with clubs, sticks, and axes (to batter out doors and windows, one presumes, since there were no plans to injure Jerry's captors) were readied for action. Reverend Loguen and others carried a battering ram. A federal marshal fired several shots into the crowd, wounding one, before retreating. To save himself, he jumped through a window into the Erie Canal, breaking his arm in the fall.

The crowd battered down the cell door, rescued the fugitive, and took him to safe quarters, where he remained for five days while recovering from beatings he had received from the police. Jerry probably yelled about police brutality too. When he was sufficiently recovered to travel, he was spirited away to Canada.

The abolitionists of Syracuse then showed their contempt for the Fugitive Slave Law by sending President Fillmore "a box, by express, containing Jerry's shackles." And they had other plans.

Reverend May remembered that the ladies of Syracuse presented James R. Lawrence, a retired judge serving as United States attorney for New York, a reward for his part in the Jerry affair: "30 pieces of silver—(3 cent pieces)—the price of betraying innocent blood." (The reference is to Jesus being betrayed by his disciple Judas, as told in Matthew 26: 14–16.) Judas killed himself after betraying Jesus. Judge Lawrence, apparently unmoved by the thirty pieces of silver he received from the ladies of Syracuse, went on with his official duties.

As Albert J. von Frank related in his masterful *The Trials of Anthony Burns*, Fillmore and Webster "were determined to make an example of the rescuers and directed the U.S. attorney for New York, James R. Lawrence, . . . to bring treason charges." In all, twenty-six men were charged, including the Reverends Ward and Loguen, both of whom escaped to Canada. As former slaves, they were in special danger if they chose to remain in Syracuse and await trial. It is reasonable to assume they did not wish to be martyrs, but their flight was not that of a classic disobedient who would accept punishment for his actions.

The citizens of Syracuse apparently protected the rescuers as best they could, for evidence against the mob was difficult to gather. Four of the men were finally tried, three whites and one black. The outcome indicates that racism was not dead in New York. The three whites were exonerated. As von Frank pointedly noted, "the lone black defendant, Enoch Reed, was convicted under the Fugitive Slave Act of 1793," a conviction that may be seen as "utterly defeating the political aim of vindicating the law of 1850."

The civil disobedient actions of the Vigilance Committee and its supporters in Syracuse were effective. As Gerrit Smith remarked at the planning committee before the second episode at the police station, "A forcible rescue will demonstrate the strength of public opinion against the possible legality of slavery, and this Fugitive Slave Law in particular. It will honor Syracuse and be a powerful example everywhere." Abolitionists wanted and needed powerful examples.

LOUIS

One of the most unusual Fugitive Slave Law cases to be heard in Cincinnati after the passage of the 1850 law concerned a slave named Louis. The episode, occurring in October 1853, was filled with acts of civil disobedience and was entirely nonviolent, not surprisingly because the Quaker Levi Coffin (1798–1877), the so-called president of the Underground Railroad, was heavily involved. Details of the following account are taken from Coffin's *Reminiscences*.

Louis had escaped from central Kentucky several years earlier, and had lived in Cincinnati for a time before moving on to Columbus, Ohio. But Louis's owner located him and traveled to Columbus to reclaim his long-absent slave. After his arrest, the federal marshal, the owner, and Louis departed by train for Cincinnati and then Kentucky. Friends of Louis telegraphed Cincinnati attorney John Jolliffe, who represented many escaped slaves and often worked with Coffin in abolitionist activities. Jolliffe immediately called on Coffin to plan strategy. These two, while the train was making its way toward the Ohio River, secured a writ charging the master with kidnapping. He was arrested when the three men arrived at the Little Miami railroad station.

Jolliffe and a fellow attorney decided on the defense: Louis, they charged, had been brought years earlier into Ohio by his master; according to Ohio law, the slave was now legally free. Louis's master was released from jail to return to Kentucky to gather materials for his case, and Louis was jailed awaiting his trial. When Louis's owner returned, the case was heard by Commissioner Carpenter. Testimony went on for several days before the commissioner was ready to render his decision. The room was crowded with blacks and whites who supported Louis, some pro-slavery people, and others merely curious. The abolitionists had no plans to create confusion and rush Louis out of the room.

"The judge," Coffin wrote, "was slow and tedious in reviewing the evidence" and spoke in a low voice. Everyone was intent on trying to hear what he was saying. Louis was sitting between his master and the marshal from Columbus. Coffin continues his story: "Louis was crowded, and to gain more room, slipped his chair back a little way. Neither his master nor the marshal noticed the movement . . . and he slipped his chair again, until he was back of them." Coffin was watching the entire scene as Louis was among sympathizers, and one put a good hat on him to give him a disguise. Eventually turning around, Louis made his way through a group of German observers. Germans were typically anti-slavery advocates; they did not betray Louis, who saw an opportunity to escape and quickly acted on it. He made his way into the street, and since he was familiar with the city, he knew of an escape route. He sought refuge with the sexton of a black cemetery.

Louis was not missed for five minutes! The Columbus marshal then called out, "Louis is gone," and he and the pro-slavery contingent rushed into the street and began a futile search for the escapee.

Coffin and some of his fellow abolitionists felt that Louis was not safe with the sexton, and the next night they disguised Louis as a woman and took him to the home of a black friend. Coffin's wife was probably responsible for supplying the dress and accessories. Louis stayed in a locked room for a week, only two or three people aware of his whereabouts. Coffin believed that Louis was still in danger, for police were seen in the neighborhood. Louis was moved once more, again disguised as a woman on her way to evening services at a nearby church. With Coffin leading the way and Louis following a short distance behind, the runaway slave was brought to the basement of a church where the trustees were sympathetic. Because the search for him continued, he remained in hiding in the church for several weeks.

The marshal from Columbus disguised himself as a Quaker and moved among Friends settlements in that part of Ohio, pretending to have great concern for the runaway slave. He learned nothing.

Meanwhile Coffin, who liked to plant false or misleading clues as he helped fugitive slaves escape, was undoubtedly the perpetrator of a hoax that he later noted: "A telegram was sent to Cincinnati from Columbus and published in the *Gazette*, saying that Louis had passed there on the train bound for Cleveland, and another dispatch from Cleveland, saying he arrived there and [had] taken the boat for Detroit." Louis remained in the church basement until Coffin and friends could arrange to get him on the way to Canada.

A Presbyterian minister and his wife, traveling by horse and carriage and stopping in town, offered to help. Louis was again disguised as a woman, with a veil over his face, and was seated in the back seat of the carriage with the minister's wife, the minister in the front seat driving the horse. Louis was taken thirty miles away to an Underground Railroad station and sent on to Sandusky, Ohio, and then to Canada.

Coffin reported, with relish, that Louis's owner then charged that the Columbus marshal had lost custody of the fugitive and asked for recompense of one thousand dollars. A compromise was reached, and the marshal paid eight hundred dollars. Coffin and other abolitionists would have agreed with Thoreau that men like the marshal served an immoral state, and that they should therefore have no sympathy for his financial woes. They also would have had no sympathy for the Kentucky master. He might have been paid for his escaped slave, but he had been jailed and had had his life upended by the trial and subsequent long search for Louis.

Coffin, a longtime civil disobedient of state and federal laws, was personally committed to nonviolence. He helped about three thousand slaves escape. He always used nonviolent tactics, and as far as he knew, not one of the slaves he helped was captured. His methods, he believed, were completely successful.

ANTHONY BURNS

Anthony Burns, the last of thirteen children, was born a slave in Stafford County, Virginia, probably in 1834. He belonged to the Suttle family, owners of a sandstone quarry. The Suttles were not prosperous—their property was heavily mortgaged—and they were forced to sell five of Anthony's siblings. Even after those sales, the Suttles owned more slaves than they had work for, so they hired out the services of Anthony and his mother and sister. Anthony was hired out several times; while working at a sawmill he was so seriously injured that a bone protruded through the skin of his right wrist. He did not receive proper medical attention, and that injury was still noticeable in Boston after his escape.

Tony, as he was called, learned to read when he was seven, but his reading skills were not great. He did, however, read the Bible, and from an early age he was religious. He became a lay preacher, ministering to fellow slaves in his neighborhood— a dangerous practice since whites were likely to take action to stop him. He also began to teach his fellow slaves to read, an activity strictly forbidden. Thus he was an active civil disobedient, defying the laws of Virginia.

Hired out to a druggist in Richmond, Burns scouted the docks. In late January 1854, with the help of a Northern sailor, he stowed away on a ship bound for Boston. With severe storms at sea, Burns had an uncomfortable, cold voyage, lengthened to three weeks. He probably reached Boston on February 19.

Little is known about his early months in Boston. He worked at various odd jobs before being arrested as a fugitive slave the night of May 24. He was arraigned the next day, and his master came to Boston for the hearing.

The Vigilance Committee immediately offered help to the frightened Burns, but at first he spurned that assistance. The attorney Richard Henry Dana wrote, "He is a piteous object, rather weak in mind. . . . He seemed completely cowed and disspirited." Burns was afraid that his master Suttle would treat him more harshly if he resisted returning to Virginia.

Burns's hearing before the commissioner was delayed, giving the Vigilance Committee more time to plan strategy. To give public support, they printed and posted this provocative handbill:

KIDNAPPING

AGAIN!!

A MAN WAS STOLEN LAST NIGHT BY THE

FUGITIVE SLAVE BILL COMMISSIONER!

HE WILL HAVE HIS

MOCK TRIAL

ON SATURDAY, MAY 27, AT 9 O'CLOCK

In the Kidnapper's 'Court,'
before the Hon. Slave Bill Commissioner

AT THE COURT HOUSE, IN COURT SQUARE.

SHALL BOSTON STEAL ANOTHER MAN?

Thursday, May 25, 1854.

The Vigilance Committee members, though they recognized that Burns would probably be returned to slavery, wanted to support his cause. The committee was large—about sixty members—of widely differing views. Some wanted to create confusion in the courtroom, as had been done during Shadrach's rescue. Others wanted to make a direct assault on the courthouse and the guards. Some held to the vain hope of a successful legal defense to free Burns. William Lloyd Garrison kept to his principles of nonresistance and was largely aloof from the Vigilance Committee's activist plans. The abolitionist Quaker poet John Greenleaf Whittier proposed a tactic later used by Mahatma Gandhi and Dr. Martin Luther King, Jr.: a peaceful march. He wrote, "If you want the country to march into Boston, say so at once." The Vigilance Committee did not choose that approach.

The story of the conflicts within the Vigilance Committee over the Burns case is long and complex, compellingly told by Albert J. von Frank. For our purposes, it is sufficient to say that the decision to attack the well-guarded courthouse where Burns was housed was poorly planned and executed.

On the night of May 26 a crowd of perhaps five hundred blacks and whites filled the square in front of the courthouse. Bricks were thrown, and violence was in the air. There were cries of "Take him out!" "Rescue him!" "Where is he?"

Axes were being used to try to break open an outside door of the courthouse. Then men with a battering ram appeared (a reprisal of Jerry's second rescue). The carriers were the abolitionist minister Thomas Wentworth Higginson, Lewis Hayden (who had helped organize the failed attempt to rescue Sims), and the attorney Seth Webb, Jr. They battered a small opening in the door and a black man sprang in, followed by Higginson, then another black man. Guards were in the hallway, and in the struggle the young Irish-born James Batchelder was killed by one of the attackers, identity unknown.

The courthouse guards proved to be a superior force, and the Burns rescue squad fell back in defeat. The crowd in the square began to dissipate, and Higginson yelled to them, "You cowards, will you desert us now?"

But the rescue attempt was over.

The legal battle to save Burns continued for a time but failed, and the commissioner ordered Burns returned to Virginia. There were, however, peaceful protests. Burns's master was in Boston for the hearing and was staying in a hotel. Blacks held a twenty-four-hour nonviolent protest vigil on the sidewalk in front of the hotel. On the day that Burns was marched through the city to the ship, many store owners draped their shops in black. Others hung the American flag upside down.

Burns was returned to his native state where he was, as he feared, badly treated. He was sold and moved to North Carolina. Funds were raised to purchase his freedom, and in late February 1855 he returned north. He studied theology at Oberlin and was later a pastor in Indiana. He moved to Canada and was a minister there until his death on July 27, 1862.

In the three decades before the Civil War, abolitionists were often reviled. In 1847, for example, Anthony Bryant, a free black living on a farm near Newman, Illinois, wanted help in getting his slave wife and her children away from their owner. Bryant was a lay preacher, and he thought the Reverend William Watson of Camargo, Illinois, might help a fellow religious man. Watson, though, was a candidate for a seat in the state legislature and did not wish to damage his political chances by being called an abolitionist. He wished Bryant well, promised to pray for Bryant's family, but asked the black man never to mention the visit. Bryant did get help from an Oakland, Illinois, physician, Dr. Hiram Rutherford, an abolitionist who did not fear for his views to be known. Dr. Rutherford helped the Bryant family escape, was sued by their owner, and in the second trial Abraham Lincoln represented the slaveowner. The doctor won the case, and the Bryants were freed. The pro-slavery element in east central Illinois had many adherents, and during the second trial there were threats of violence. Abolitionists were most often scorned in this area with its many Southern supporters, but Dr. Rutherford was unafraid of anti-abolition sentiments.

Southern newspaper editors were apoplectic on the subject of abolitionists and "slave stealers." And many of the people in free states who disapproved of slavery nonetheless disliked the disruptive tactics employed by many abolitionists. On the attempt to rescue Anthony Burns, the *Boston Journal* on May 30, 1854, wrote, echoing the views of the

now-deceased Webster: "The abolitionists and their confederates did all they could to subserve the cause of mob law! . . .
What these bold, bad men are doing, is nothing more nor less
than committing treason."

The Massachusetts public, though, had trouble justifying
Burns's return to slavery. He was a religious man, a lay
preacher. He was willing to work. Bostonians were faced with
the question: Had the federal government turned tyrannical
when it insisted on keeping such persons enslaved?

Thoreau had proposed a way to oppose tyranny—to follow a "higher law," break the laws supporting slavery, and accept the punishment of jail for acts of civil disobedience. He
was bitterly offended by the arrest of Burns and other fugitive
slaves and was prompted to write "Slavery in Massachusetts,"
an indictment of the citizens of his state who did not intervene
to stop the reenslavement of fugitives. In his earlier essay
"Civil Disobedience," Thoreau wrote in rather generalized
terms about the evils of government, but in "Slavery in Massachusetts" he was more specific: "My thoughts are murder to
the State." He argued that the Fugitive Slave Law of 1850 per-
petuated grave injustice to several million enslaved, and he attacked the people of the state of Massachusetts who supported
that law. His radical idea was succinct: "The law will never
make men free; it is men who have got to make the law free.
They are the lovers of law and order, who observe the law
when the government breaks it." Thoreau was not repudiating
civil disobedience, but he was becoming more of an activist.

Thoreau delivered "Slavery in Massachusetts" as a lecture
at Framingham, Massachusetts, on July 4, 1854. It was widely
praised, and a shortened version appeared in the *Liberator* on
July 21. At the same July 4 meeting, William Lloyd Garrison
read the Declaration of Independence and then contrasted it

with the Constitution of the United States which made slavery legal. This was followed by a reading of documents supporting the return of Burns to Virginia. Garrison then burned the offending documents individually, sparing the Declaration of Independence, saying in each case, "So perish all compromises with tyranny. And let all the people say *Amen!*"

Although Webster died in 1852, his view that those who broke the law and helped fugitive slaves should be subject to prosecution remained strong federal policy. Some of those identified as participating in the Burns case were charged in federal court, others in state court. But with or without Webster urging prosecution and conviction, juries in Boston refused to convict. The defendants had good legal representation, but there was a growing sympathy for escaped slaves and a suspicion that the government was controlled by slaveowners. All such prosecutions following the Burns case failed.

Supporters of Burns might have used civil disobedience tactics and gained more public support, but they blundered into violence and the killing of one person. Not one of the defendants appeared ready to go to jail, as Thoreau had done, on a matter of principle.

DRED SCOTT

Dred Scott, a Missouri slave, was taken by his army physician owner Dr. John Emerson into free territories. Scott then sued for his freedom, his attorneys arguing that since he had lived where slavery was forbidden, he should be set free. The case made its way to the United States Supreme Court in 1856, and the decision, written by Chief Justice Roger Brooke Taney (1777–1864), was announced the following year. Taney had been born into a wealthy slaveowning family in Maryland,

and had been appointed to the Court in 1836. In the 1850s his rulings supported advocates of slavery. He upheld the Fugitive Slave Laws, denying the rights of free states to refuse to obey those laws.

The Dred Scott decision, on a 7-2 vote, greatly inflamed the already tense sectional conflict over slavery. Taney, speaking for the majority, ruled that Scott could not sue in federal court because blacks were not citizens and had no rights. Reflecting the racism of his time, he wrote, "They had for more than a century before been regarded as beings of an inferior order; and altogether unfit to associate with the white race, either in social or political relations; and so far inferior that they had no rights which the white man was bound to respect; and that the negro might justly and lawfully be reduced to slavery for his benefit."

The Court in this decision also ruled that Congress could not pass such legislation as the Missouri Compromise of 1820 or the Kansas-Nebraska Act of 1854, for such legislation prevented owners from taking slaves into any territory.

Pro-slavery forces in the country won an important legal victory in the Dred Scott decision, but in free states where some people were concerned about the fate of escaped slaves, an increasing number of citizens were troubled by a ruling they considered inhumane. The decision encouraged violence on all sides; nonviolence as a tactic to abolish slavery was now little discussed. The violent attack by John Brown in 1859 at Harpers Ferry was almost a death blow to the movement for civil disobedience and nonviolence. Even Thoreau defended John Brown.

FROM THE CIVIL WAR

THROUGH RECONSTRUCTION:

THE END OF SLAVERY

Joshua fit de battle of Jericho,
Jericho, Jericho,
Joshua fit de battle of Jericho,
And de walls come tumbling down.
—From "Joshua Fit de Battle of Jericho"

❦ In 1860, Abraham Lincoln was elected president of a divided country, riven with decades of sectional strife. Even before he took office, South Carolina seceded from the Union, to be followed soon after by Mississippi, Florida, Alabama, Georgia, Louisiana, Texas, Arkansas, North Carolina, Virginia, and Tennessee. Four border states—Delaware, Maryland, Kentucky, and Missouri—remained in the Union. Early on, Lincoln maintained that his goal was to preserve the Union, not destroy slavery, and he was slow to move toward emancipation.

Slaves, though, took advantage of the confusion of a long civil war, 1861–1865, to flee behind Union lines, declaring

Fugitive slaves fording the Rappahannock River during the Civil War, August 1862. *(Wallach Division, New York Public Library)*

civil disobedience against their owners, local slave codes, and the Confederacy of secessionist Southern states.

At Fort Monroe in Virginia, Union General Benjamin Butler, learning in the spring of 1861 that some black refugees were helping build Union defenses, declared that they were "contraband of war" and would not be returned to their owners. The response of other Union generals was often quite different; several wanted to return all escaped slaves to their owners. General George B. McClellan in May 1861 assured Virginia slaveholders, "Not only will we abstain from all interference with your slaves, but we will, with an iron hand, crush any attempt at insurrection on their part." General

Ulysses S. Grant in 1862 in Tennessee ordered escaped slaves returned to owners who supported the Union cause. Runaway slaves belonging to Confederate supporters were set to work building Union fortifications.

On August 6, 1861, Congress passed the First Confiscation Act. Slaves who were used to benefit the Confederate cause could be seized by Union forces and set free. General John C. Frémont then announced the freeing of all slaves belonging to Missouri Confederates, going far beyond the terms of the act. Lincoln countermanded Frémont's order, insisting that only those slaves used in activities supporting the Confederacy should be freed.

As the war progressed, slaves who had not fled began to believe they would be freed. The diarist Mary Chestnut wrote that her butler, a slave she had taught to read, was "inscrutably silent" and "won't look at me now. He looks over my head, he scents freedom in the air."

Many slaveholders who had clung to the belief, against all evidence, that their slaves were treated benevolently and would be loyal to their owners appeared shocked when seemingly docile slaves suddenly took advantage of wartime confusion and fled. Emily Douglass of Natchez, Mississippi, complained that her slaves "left without even a good-bye." She was fortunate that there were no threats from or confrontations with her slaves before they left.

Slaves by the thousands and then the tens of thousands declared civil disobedience against their owners and the Confederacy and fled behind Union lines, often at great peril to themselves. Levi Coffin visited several of the "contraband" camps along the Ohio and Mississippi rivers and interviewed many escapees. He wrote in his *Reminiscences*: "As the slaveholders fled before the advancing Union forces they took with them their able-bodied slaves, and when these tried to escape and reach the Union lines, they were pursued and fired upon by their masters who had rather shoot them down than let them go free."

Charlotte Forten, granddaughter of James Forten, a prominent black abolitionist, went in 1862 to teach on St. Helena, one of the South Carolina Sea Islands. The Union navy had captured the Sea Islands, and the Confederate slaveholders had fled, leaving many blacks behind. Charlotte Forten wrote about a civil disobedient act by an escaping slave. The incident began nonviolently but was turned violent by the slaveowner: "15 of the people on this place escaped from the main land, last spring. Among them was a man named Michael. After they had gone some distance—their master in pursuit—M[ichael]'s master overtook him in the swamp. A fierce grapple ensued—the master on horseback, the man on foot:—the former drew a pistol and shot the slave through the arm, shattering it dreadfully. Still the brave man fought desperately and at last succeeded in unhorsing the master, and beat him until he was senseless. He then with the rest of the company escaped."

The Union navy captured Port Royal in the Sea Islands in November 1861, and Union General Rufus Saxton reported on the Confederate slaveholders and their slaves: the planters "tried to take their negroes with them [deeper into Confederate territory], but they would not go. They shot down their negroes in many instances because they would not go with them. They tied them behind their wagons and tried to drag them off; but the negroes would not go. The great majority of negroes [80 percent] remained behind and came into our lines."

The government in Washington did not have adequate plans to care for these thousands of civil disobedients who op-

posed the Confederate government that was fighting to keep
them enslaved. Washington politicians did not provide sufficient funds to care for these refugees. Everywhere Levi Coffin
went in his trips to the "contraband" camps, he found "great
destitution and suffering," and most contrabands living without proper housing or food. Coffin began to work to collect
food, supplies, money, and books for the refugees, as tempo-
rary schools were also being established to meet the needs of
the large numbers of slaves who wanted to learn to read. Coffin did find that the superintendents in charge of the camps
were coping as best they could with limited resources.

Harriet Jacobs, the escaped slave and author of *Incidents in
the Life of a Slave Girl*, went to Virginia to work with contrabands. She too found the same "great destitution and suffering" noted by Coffin, but in Alexandria she also found the
activities of one of the aid workers reprehensible. Reverend Albert Gladwin of the New York American Baptist Free Mission
Society was charged with mistreating the contrabands,
"threatening to flog them & scolding them as if they were animals," according to a Quaker co-worker of Jacobs. His actions seemed like those of a slave driver. With the support of
military authorities, he declared that the barracks where the
poverty-stricken refugees were living rent free would hence-
forth be rented to those who could pay. When Gladwin was
appointed superintendent of the refugee camp, he continued
his mistreatment of contrabands. Jacobs protested his actions,
and the Freedmen's Relief Association filed complaints against
him similar to the objections lodged by Jacobs. She noted that
the refugees felt "their condition was made worse by being
made free. Their present master is the hardest master of their
lives." The army investigated and completely exonerated Gladwin, though he was eventually dismissed. The mistreatment of

contrabands by officials foreshadowed many of the problems blacks were to face in the years ahead.

Levi Coffin wrote about the differences between black contrabands and a group of three hundred Southern white civil disobedient refugees, a story with Chekhovian overtones. Coffin had been visiting contraband camps in the South, and on a ship going upriver on the Mississippi he observed a large group of mostly white women and children refugees. They were, he wrote in his *Reminiscences*, "wretched" and "forlorn-looking." He discovered that these people had been disloyal to the Confederacy, and he continued: "They had been ruined by the war, being Unionists in sentiment and opposed to secession, their property had been destroyed or taken by the rebels, their houses burned, and the men forced to flee for their lives or enter the rebel service." Coffin does not identify these people further, but many of them were probably descendants of German and other northern Europeans who had farms and ranches in the South but did not own slaves; or they might have been mountain people from the Carolinas, Virginia, and Tennessee who opposed slavery. "The husbands and fathers of some of these families had been shot down before their eyes," Coffin discovered when he interviewed many of them after they had landed in Cairo, Illinois. They were being sent to Illinois and Indiana to be housed with people who would take them in, but their situation was tragic, some lying without protection on the wet ground, others wandering around in "a dejected and spiritless manner."

Coffin concluded, "I had witnessed many scenes of destitution and suffering among the contrabands in the South, but this surpassed them all. The colored people were hopeful; they had gained their liberty, and in the midst of privation and hardship were praising the Lord for their deliverance from bondage. The [white] refugees were despondent, and many of them wept bitterly as they related their sad stories."

Contraband slaves and white Unionists in the South all suffered greatly as a result of their civil disobedience.

Patriotic blacks in the free states, undoubtedly wanting to help destroy the slave system, hoped to enlist in the Union army, but Lincoln's secretary of war refused: "This department has no intention at the present to call into the service of the government any colored soldiers." Some black men with light complexions declared civil disobedience and joined Northern fighting units anyway. Officers no doubt knew of the subterfuge and chose to ignore the secretary of war.

After continuing pressure to enlist black men, Congress passed the Second Confiscation Act and Militia Act of 1862, authorizing President Lincoln to accept black men into military service. On January 1, 1863, the First South Carolina Volunteer Regiment of black soldiers was brought into the Union army, followed by the Second South Carolina Volunteers, the 54th Massachusetts Regiment, the 14th Rhode Island Heavy Artillery Regiment, and several others.

Black soldiers faced many problems, illustrated by the difficulties of Rhode Island's Corporal Cravat. In the violence-filled environment of war, he contemplated violence after black troops were mistreated by riotous New Orleans police. He was also, in the Thoreau mode, a nonviolent civil disobedient who refused to accept lower, discriminatory pay and went to jail as a matter of principle.

John A. Cravat (1831–1897), a free black barber from Woonsocket, Rhode Island, was married and had three children when in the spring of 1863 he enlisted as a private in the black 14th Rhode Island Heavy Artillery Regiment, Company

A, First Battalion. Cravat's unit arrived in New Orleans on December 29, 1863, for a five-day stay. He remained on ship the first two days, then he and friends spent the next day exploring the city. After they returned, he wrote his wife on January 10, 1864: ". . . the Police came down to the bote and kicked up a fuss with some of the boys that was standing on the dock. The Police fired a pistol. That was a nuff—the boys started for them and for one hour things was hot. Our boys beat one so bad that he died. It seems as tho a Friday nite there was a Ball and some of our boys was there and the Police made a rush to arrest them, and in the attempt one of the Police got a hole in him that left the wind all out. So a Saturday afternoon they came to the bote for revenge but got saddely disipinted [disappointed] and drove off. They tried to shoot our Major, and if they had New Orleans today would lay in ashes. . . ."

Cravat later offered further views on the New Orleans conflict in a letter to his wife from Fort Esperanza in Texas, dated February 10: "The truth is this—the Police became riotous because we were not kept on shipboard and dared to come ashore and walk the streets of New Orleans like men. . . . The truth is they hate free blacks and all connected with them. . . . They say they don't want to see any more free long booted neggers there again. . . ." Cravat felt that the action against the police was self-protection on the part of the free black soldiers.

His act of civil disobedience concerned his pay. According to the Enlistment Act of 1862, white privates were to receive $13 a month plus $3.50 for a clothing allotment; blacks were to receive $7 and $3 for clothing. In 1864, Corporal Cravat and seventeen of his black colleagues in Company A, First Battalion, demanded equal pay. He explained to his wife in a letter of April 29: "You will see by my letter that I am today in New Orleans. I and 17 others arrived here yesterday as pris-

oners." Because of their demand for equal pay, the black soldiers were court-martialed and sentenced to jail for sticking up
for their rights. He continued, "We have been in the service
8 months yesterday and have not received any monthly pay."
He believed that receiving a lesser amount of pay than that
given to white privates was discriminatory: "there have not
been any provisions made by congress where colored soldiers
can get the same pay as white soldiers. This is the biggest hum-
bug I ever had anything to do with and it ought to be brought
before the Publick."

Although he had suffered this discrimination by the War
Department, Cravat supported the war effort. He wrote his
wife from the New Orleans police jail on May 16: "I have bin
here two weeks last friday and I am even glad I am here for today I stan in a free state. Yes the City of N.O. is a free City.
Who would of thought this five or six months ago that the
State of Louisiana could boast of having thrown off the yoak
of bondage."

Other black army units protested salary discrimination, and
later in 1864 the War Department granted equal pay to blacks.
Corporal Cravat and the seventeen other civil disobedients were
freed, and all received back pay at the basic thirteen-dollar rate.
Cravat received an honorable discharge in April 1865.

Slaves fought the Confederacy in both nonviolent and violent
ways, as shown by Robert Smalls's audacious theft of the
steamer *Planter* from Charleston, liberating sixteen people in
all. The act was nonviolent, but the escaping men would have
been dealt with harshly had they been captured by Confederate officials.

Robert Smalls (1839–1915), one of the most famous of the
civil disobedients opposing the Confederacy, was born a slave

Robert Smalls piloted the steamer *Planter* to freedom and liberated sixteen people. *(National Archives)*

in Beaufort, South Carolina, to Lydia, a house servant in the home of John McKee, who was probably Robert's father. As a small child Robert was a "houseboy," known for his intelligence and "kind disposition." He did not have a harsh life in the McKee household, but he was aware of the cruelties around him. He saw slaves in stocks for twenty-four or forty-eight hours with heavy weights attached to their legs. He observed a slave with an "iron collar with two prongs sticking out at the sides like cow's horns."

His childhood ended when he was twelve. He was taken from his mother and sent to live with Charleston relatives of his master. There he was set to work as a waiter, later a lamplighter, and then a stevedore. At seventeen he married Hannah Jones, a slave who worked as a hotel maid. Hannah was thirty-one, and it appears not to have been a love match. Smalls seems to have married to gain stability in his life. "My idea," he said, "was to have a wife to prevent me running around—to have someone to do for me and to keep me." He gained a wife and a mother, and Hannah does seem to have helped him mature.

Smalls apparently had some kind of business as a sideline to his stevedore work. He paid his owner fifteen dollars a month and kept everything else he earned. He paid his wife's owner five dollars a month as a condition of permitting her to marry. After his daughter was born in 1858, he made arrangements to buy his wife and daughter for eight hundred dollars; he had saved seven hundred dollars at the time of the escape.

In 1861, after several years of working on the Charleston docks, he became a deckhand on the *Planter*, a wooden steamer 147 feet long and displacing 300 tons. She was a sidewheeler that burned wood. At the time Smalls joined the crew, the *Planter* was engaged in commercial trade, largely devoted to moving cotton bales in the Charleston area. In March 1861 the Confederacy chartered the steamer to carry munitions and other materiel throughout the Charleston vicinity with its various fortifications. By the next year the intelligent Smalls seems to have been acting as wheelman—that is, the pilot—of the *Planter*. He began to think of escape; he said in a speech after he went missing from the Confederacy, "Although born a slave I always felt that I was a man and ought to be free, and I would be free or die." He was echoing Thoreau's statement: "I think that it is not too soon for honest men to rebel and revolutionize"—though Smalls had not read "Civil Disobedience."

About two weeks before the theft of the *Planter*, Smalls began to make plans to flee. Three white men were assigned to the steamer—Captain C. J. Relyea, Mate Samuel H. Smith, and engineer Zerich Pitcher—and the remaining crew was black. Smalls must have noted that the three white men did not follow military regulations, for they all would leave together to spend the night on the town. He began to ask the black crew about joining him in hijacking the *Planter*; some were frightened about the penalties they and their families would suffer should they be captured, and they declined. Seven men agreed to join him, and he offered to those with wives and children that they could be brought along.

Smalls asked his wife if she were willing to take the risk of fleeing with him. Echoing the Book of Ruth 1:16–17, Hannah responded, "I will go, . . . for where you die I will die." Hannah and the two children—a son had been recently born— would join him in the attempt to gain their freedom.

On the night of May 12, 1862, Relyea, Smith, and Pitcher left the *Planter* for a night of revelry. After their departure, Smalls used some of his time to contact crew members, wives, and children about plans to escape that very night. At 3 a.m. on May 13, Smalls was in control of the *Planter*, which was armed with a cannon and a howitzer. The already-loaded cargo to be delivered that day consisted of four guns plus a guncarriage, items to be offloaded at Fort Ripley and Fort Sumter. The crew fired the boiler, and Smalls hoisted the Confederate and South Carolina flags.

The steamer moved away from the dock, heading for the North Atlantic wharf, where Smalls's wife and two children and others boarded. Eight men, five women, and three children were aboard. The *Planter* was slowed by the incoming tide. Everything needed to appear normal in this escape. The crew had to appear to be doing regular duties; the wives and children had to stay below deck at all times. Smalls and the crew may have had a contingency plan for using the cannons on board in the event their plot was discovered.

Smalls acted a part as if in a play. He put on the captain's large straw hat, dressed in some of the captain's clothes, and stood in the window of the pilothouse, his arms folded, just as Captain Relyea habitually stood.

Smalls now took the *Planter* down the South Channel. A skilled pilot, he knew the waters, and he knew the appropriate signals to the guards. At Fort Johnson he gave the correct whistle signal. When the *Planter* reached Fort Sumter, Smalls again gave the correct whistle signal, and it was acknowledged. The *Planter* was allowed to continue. A morning haze probably helped keep the guards at Forts Johnson and Sumter from recognizing that a black man wearing a large straw hat was in the pilothouse.

Smalls then ran up a white flag. He knew that the Union fleet blockading the Charleston harbor might fire on the ship. That was indeed the case. A lookout on the Union vessel *Onward* thought the *Planter* was a wooden ship sent out to ram one of the Union ships, and the *Onward* was brought into position to fire. A Union sailor then saw through the haze a white flag, and the *Planter* was allowed to come alongside the *Onward*. Union sailors could then see that all aboard the *Planter* were black, and some were "singing, some whistling, jumping . . . and muttering all sorts of maledictions" against Fort Sumter in the background.

Taken aboard the *Onward*, Smalls removed his hat and said lines he must have been rehearsing in the pilothouse: "Good morning, sir! I've brought you some of the old United States guns, sir." Smalls had actually brought much more: the *Planter*, used by Union forces the rest of the war; documents aboard the steamer; and Smalls's knowledge of the waters. He knew, for example, where mines had been placed around Charleston harbor.

Smalls became a Union hero and spoke to cheering audiences in the North. He served as a pilot and then captain in the last years of the war. He spent much of the rest of his life as a South Carolina Republican political figure, serving five terms in the House of Representatives in Washington. For many years he was collector of customs in Beaufort.

Smalls liberated sixteen people, an act of civil disobedience widely condemned in South Carolina. The *Columbia Guardian* wished that the "recreant parties will be brought to speedy justice, and the prompt penalty of the halter rigorously enforced." But the sixteen contrabands were beyond the reach of Confederate "justice."

Under pressure, President Lincoln finally announced the Emancipation Proclamation to take effect January 1, 1863, freeing all slaves in the rebellious states. The 800,000 slaves in border states that did not join the Confederacy were not affected at that time. The Confederacy, of course, did not recognize the Emancipation Proclamation, and slavery continued to be practiced in all the breakaway states from the Union.

With the end of the war and the passage of the Thirteenth Amendment in 1865, all blacks were at last free. After decades of struggle, the abolitionists had triumphed—or so it seemed for a time. With the assassination of Lincoln on April 14, 1865, Andrew Johnson from Tennessee assumed the presidency and began to allow Southern whites to assume control of their states.

Almost immediately the former slave states began to pass legislation similar to the Black Codes of earlier times. Blacks were restricted in purchasing or renting property, forced to work, and could be imprisoned if they quit their positions. They were not allowed to testify in court against whites, and ways were found to deny blacks the right to vote.

An ominous development began slowly after the end of the war. The Ku Klux Klan, a robed, hooded group of white supremacists, was organized in Pulaski, Tennessee, in late 1865 and early 1866, to intimidate blacks. At first the members seemed like Halloween pranksters in outrageous costumes as they attempted to frighten newly freed blacks. Sometimes the intimidation worked, but many blacks saw through the stage effects and recognized the voices of their former masters or local businessmen. Early on, the Klan was not the powerful, violent force it would later become.

Angered by President Johnson's policies, abolitionists and their friends in Congress began to confront him and press for major changes in his approach to the defeated South. Senator Charles Sumner of Massachusetts, Representative Thaddeus Stevens of Pennsylvania, and their allies known as Radical Republicans began to legislate their own Reconstruction plans, which disfranchised many former Confederates and placed the South under military rule. Blacks voted and elected blacks to local, state, and national offices. The Fourteenth Amendment was ratified on July 21, 1868. It begins: "No State shall make or enforce any law which shall abridge the privileges or immunities of citizens of the United States. . . ."

True believers in white supremacy and segregation were incensed by the changes forced on the South by Radical Republicans, and they fought back in a variety of ways. Public schools were established during Radical Reconstruction, and landowners, in particular, resented paying taxes for "schools for niggers." Male teachers were threatened, whipped, tarred and feathered, and murdered. Black schools were burned. Women

Early members of the Ku Klux Klan.
(Harper's Weekly, Library of Congress)

teachers from the North were generally sent threatening letters and forced to give up their teaching and return home.

The activities of the Ku Klux Klan, even when its raids did not end in murder, are still painful to read about after all these years, marked as they are by cruelty, hatred, and at times sexual degradation.

William Champion of Spartanburg County, South Carolina, owned land and a mill. He had been a Union man even before the war, did not serve in the Confederate army because of a leg injury, and after the war voted Republican. Worse, he treated blacks fairly, even allowing a school for black children to be built on his property. Still worse, he opposed the white power structure in South Carolina and the activities of the Klan. By all definitions he was a scalawag—a white Southerner who supported Radical Reconstruction.

Champion's visit from the Klan was predictable. His encounter with the hooded men began one fall night, when about fifty members of the Klan broke down his door, firing as they entered his house.

"Get up, you damned radical son of a bitch," they yelled. A friend staying with Champion was shot in the shoulder. The two captured men were tied and marched toward the Broad River, where the Klansmen threatened to drown Champion.

That same night another Klan group broke into the home of a black couple, the Clem Bowdens. Bowden was a successful carpenter and had been able to buy a small farm with twelve acres of corn and cotton in cultivation. Klan members viewed with suspicion blacks who were prospering, just as they detested scalawags such as Champion and carpetbaggers—Northerners who came south and supported Radical Reconstruction.

Bowden had also come to the attention of the Klan because he was an election manager, and he voted Republican. An ox yoke was placed on Bowden's shoulders, and he and his wife, both sixty years of age, were marched down the same road Champion was now on. At a clearing the Bowdens were stripped and beaten.

The Klansmen with Champion and friend then arrived at the same clearing, and the two Klan groups joined forces. Champion was stripped, told he would soon die, and brutally beaten, suffering many wounds and the loss of two teeth. Then Bowden was told to beat Champion, but the frightened black gave him soft blows before being struck in the head by a Klansman.

Bowden was then ordered to get on the ground, face down, legs spread, and Champion was forced to kiss his anus.

"Is he doing it? Is he doing it?" asked one Klansman.

"How do you like that for nigger equality!" said another.

Champion was then ordered to have intercourse with Mrs. Bowden. He explained that after his brutal beating, he was in no physical condition to do so. He was fortunate not to have been castrated, a punishment used by some Klansmen. The Klansmen then forced him to kiss her genitalia.

Satiated with a night of revelry, the Klansmen did not kill their victims, as they sometimes did. The prisoners were returned to their respective homes. Champion then reported the events of that night to the magistrate. The Klan, learning of this (the magistrate may well have been a member of the Klan) then sent Champion this letter: "BUSTER CHAMPION; We have been told that our visit to you was not a sufficient hint. We now notify you to leave the county within thirty days from the reception of this notice, or abide by the consequences. K.K.K." The Bowdens probably received much the same letter. Champion abandoned his land and mill and moved to the city of Spartanburg. The Bowdens abandoned their land and crops and also moved to the city. They can hardly be blamed. The next visit from the Klan would have resulted in their deaths.

In addition to kidnappings and murders, the Klansmen also regularly raped black women whose houses they invaded. As Wyn Craig Wade wrote in *The Fiery Cross*, "It was inevitable for the excitement of 'kluxing' helpless victims to carry over into sexual forms of expression." One of the examples used by Wade represents that reality: Near Raleigh, North Carolina, the daughter of a Mrs. Gilmore was beaten and repeatedly raped. Then the Klansmen set her pubic hair afire, and it was "singed to the flesh."

Blacks in the South believed for a short time that the rights of life, liberty, and the pursuit of happiness belonged to them, but they soon realized that they were being attacked and intimidated for owning land, for voting, for insisting that wages owed be paid, or for bringing legal suits against whites. Some of these attacks against blacks resulted from their preference for voting Republican at a time when Democrats were attempting to regain political and economic control. The Klan, a shadow government, attacked all those who did not follow its codes. If charges of intimidation or murder were brought against Klan members, other Klansmen provided alibis. After the accusers lost their cases, the Klan would retaliate against them. When the last federal troops were withdrawn from the South in 1877, the judges, sheriffs, and white supremacists who routinely denied justice to blacks had much more power.

The Fifteenth Amendment, ratified on March 30, 1870, appears to be unambiguous: "The right of citizens of the United States to vote shall not be denied or abridged by the United States or by any State on account of race, color, or previous condition of servitude." But with the end of the military occupation of the South, Southerners began to find ways to restrict the voting rights of blacks, eventually using poll taxes, literacy tests, and personal intimidation to circumvent that amendment. State and federal courts began to allow voting rights for blacks to be impaired or abolished.

White Republicans in the North soon began to turn away from support of the reform movements of Reconstruction, which had attempted to bring blacks to the polling stations, improve their economic situation, and foster educational opportunities. Using intimidation and force, racist politicians of the Democratic party came to power in local, state, and national elections in the former Confederate states. With the breakup of the plantations, black and white sharecroppers now found themselves at the mercy of the store owners. At the end of the year, after paying the store owner for seed, fertilizer, tools, and household items, the tenant farmers had earned nothing. Blacks were no longer slaves, but many were semi-serfs on the land. They were finding it more and more difficult to vote. Schools for their children, if they existed at all, were poorly funded. Hate groups rode at night to intimidate blacks. What could they do? Run away to a city, Southern or Northern, where they still faced discrimination? Or hunker down, smile and smile, play dumb, be invisible, seemingly defer to all white men, women, and children?

CHAPTER

VI

THOREAU'S ESSAY TRAVELS
ACROSS THE OCEANS TO GANDHI

> "We are the 'Asian dirt' to be 'heartily cursed,'
> we are 'chokeful of vice' and we 'live upon rice,'
> we are 'stinking coolies' living on the 'smell of an
> oiled rag,' we are 'the black vermin,' we are
> described in the Statute Books as 'semi-barbarous
> Asiatics, or persons belonging to the uncivilized
> races of Asia.' We 'breed like rabbits,' and a
> gentleman at a meeting lately held in Durban said
> he 'was sorry we could not be shot like them.'"
> —Mohandas K. Gandhi, on the plight of Indians
> in South Africa, 1896

W We now make an excursion to South Africa in the early twentieth century, where a developing civil disobedience campaign, led by Mohandas K. Gandhi, was influenced by Thoreau's essay on that subject. The Gandhian technique of mass civil disobedience then returned in the 1920s to the United States, where Gandhi and his methods were admired by blacks living in a segregated society. Finally, after three decades, "another Gandhi" named Martin Luther King, Jr., arrived on

the scene and helped bring about major changes in civil rights
in the South and throughout the United States.

At the turn of the twentieth century, at a time when segregation was a fact of life for blacks, especially in former
slaveholding states, a civil disobedience campaign led by
Gandhi, an obscure Indian attorney, began in South Africa.
Indians in that country were being subjected to severe mistreatment. In response, Gandhi led the protest which he
called for a time "passive resistance," then "civil disobedience." He eventually adopted the word *Satyagraha* (truth
force). His thinking, action, and philosophy were influenced
by several world religions, and by Ruskin, Socrates,
Thoreau, and Tolstoy. Gandhi later returned to India and,
bringing his South African experience to his native country,
began his *Satyagraha* campaign there to end British control
of that subcontinent. Gandhi's *Satyagraha* would later have
a great impact on the thinking and actions of Dr. Martin
Luther King, Jr., and others in the civil rights movement.

Mohandas Karamchand Gandhi of the Hindu Vaisya caste
was born in 1869 in Porbandar, India. His father served as
prime minister in the small states of Porbandar, Rajkot, and
Wankaner. The Gandhis were an important and influential
family, but they accumulated little wealth. Gandhi was especially attached to his mother, a deeply religious woman who
went to the Hindu temple daily and often fasted.

A small, bright, shy child, from an early age Mohandas developed strong ethical standards from his mother's influence.
In his first year of high school, his school was visited by Mr.
Giles, the educational inspector, who held a spelling examina-
tion which included the word "kettle." Gandhi misspelled the
word, and when his teacher suggested that he copy the word
from another student's slate, Gandhi refused. He remembered

in his *Autobiography*: "The result was that all the boys, except myself, were found to have spelt every word correctly. Only I had been stupid. The teacher tried later to bring this stupidity home to me, but without effect. I never could learn the art of 'copying.'"

At the age of thirteen, following the Indian custom of arranged marriages, he was married. He writes candidly about his adolescent marriage, which he says was passionate. He was then a jealous husband, and though he is now considered one of the greatest men of the twentieth century, he was often a failure in his treatment of his wife and children. There were strong puritanical and autocratic elements in his psychological makeup, but our concern here is the development of his philosophy of nonviolent civil disobedience.

When Gandhi finished school, he left his wife and baby and his extended family to study law in London. Travel abroad was forbidden by his caste, but he insisted on going and became an outcast. He did promise his mother not to break dietary laws and to remain a vegetarian.

In London, where he arrived in 1888 for a three-year stay, he set about acquiring many Western ways but found bland English food unsatisfying. At a vegetarian restaurant he purchased a copy of Henry S. Salt's *A Plea for Vegetarianism*, a book that convinced him to become a vegetarian not only by religious dictate but by choice. He was later to meet Salt, the humanitarian reformer and biographer of Thoreau, at meetings of the Vegetarian Society. Salt's causes, such as diet reform, the humane treatment of animals, and the simple life, were all to become important to Gandhi. At the time he had not read Thoreau.

Gandhi's course of study was not demanding, and in an unsystematic way he began to read about various world religions.

By birth a Hindu, he never made a special study of that religion. He had not, for instance, read *Bhagavad Gita* (often called the *Gita*), and some Theosophists introduced him to it through Sir Edwin Arnold's poetic translation called *The Song Celestial*, a work that greatly impressed him. He was also enthusiastic about Arnold's poetic life of Buddha called *The Light of Asia*. Some years later, in South Africa, he made special studies of the Koran.

In a Manchester vegetarian boardinghouse he met a Christian and bought a Bible from him. He was completely uninterested in the Old Testament, but the New Testament, he wrote in his *Autobiography*, "produced a different impression, especially the Sermon on the Mount which went straight to my heart. I compared it with the *Gita*. The verses, 'But I say unto you, that ye resist not evil; but whosoever shall smite thee on thy right cheek, turn to him the other also. And if any man take away thy coat let him have thy cloke too,' delighted me beyond measure. . . . My young mind tried to unify the teachings of the *Gita*, *The Light of Asia*, and the Sermon on the Mount."

Gandhi felt at ease studying religions and incorporating what he considered the best parts of each into his own religious views. All this served him well in later years when he acquired friends and supporters from Hindu, Jewish, Christian, and Muslim faiths.

His course of study completed, Gandhi returned to India in 1891 and to an event that brought home to him the reality of the color barrier in British India. His older brother, Laxmidas, was an adviser to the heir to the Porbandar throne, and Laxmidas expected to become prime minister, as his father had been. But when he was accused of giving bad advice to the prince, the English political agent lost faith in him. Gandhi had known the Englishman slightly when he was studying

Mohandas K. Gandhi arrived in South Africa in 1893 fashionably clothed as a British gentleman. *(Vithalbhai Jhaveri / GanhiServe)*

abroad, and his brother urged Gandhi to approach the agent and plead his case. Against his better judgment, Gandhi agreed to do so, but he was rudely treated and shown the door. He was later advised to "pocket the insult" if he hoped to be successful in British-ruled India. Experiencing such dismissive treatment was a moment of awakening for Gandhi, who did not aspire to be a sycophant or an intriguer. He was beginning to understand the barriers Indians faced.

Shy and still inexperienced in his profession, Gandhi was unable to establish a satisfactory law practice in India. When a firm of Porbandar Muslim merchants asked him to go to South Africa for a year to settle a difficult legal matter, he agreed, leaving behind his wife and two sons, the second of whom had only recently been born.

Gandhi arrived in Durban, Natal, in the spring of 1893, fashionably dressed in a frock coat, trousers, shoes, and a turban. There he quickly learned about the troubles of Indians in South Africa. Since 1860, white South Africans—British and Dutch—had been importing indentured Indian laborers to work in the growing of sugar cane, tea, and coffee. After a term of five years, the Indians were released from indenture. Many did not return to India but bought small properties and began to grow vegetables and fruit for the local markets. Indian traders and merchants also began arriving to do business with Indian farmers and with the Zulus and other black tribes in the provinces. Because both the small farmers and merchants were so successful, they drew the wrath of the white population and suffered resulting intimidation.

Both the Boers (Dutch colonists) and the British discriminated against Indians in South Africa. Dutch colonists had begun to settle in the Cape Province in the mid-seventeenth century. Early in the nineteenth century the British annexed that territory. The Boers, to escape British domination, departed on the Great Trek (1835–1840) and established the Boer republics of the Orange Free State and the Transvaal. But the British controlled commerce and the profitable mining industry, and continuing conflict between the two colonizers led to the Boer War (1899–1902), won by the British. They established the Union of South Africa in 1910 with the provinces of the Cape of Good Hope, Natal, the Orange Free State, and the Transvaal having dominion status. During Gandhi's stay in South Africa, from 1893 to 1914, political developments were complex. Attempts to alleviate discrimination against Indians often meant that Gandhi had to negotiate with both British and Boer officials—often still bitter enemies.

No matter their economic condition or profession, Indians were called "samis" or "coolies." Gandhi was known as a "coolie barrister."

A week after his arrival, Gandhi was sent by his employer to Pretoria on legal business. He booked a first-class ticket on the night train.

When the train made a stop in Maritzburg, the capital of Natal, a passenger entered the compartment occupied by Gandhi, looked him over, and seeing that he was "colored," withdrew. The passenger soon returned with two railway officials.

"Come along, you must go to the van compartment," Gandhi was told.

"But I have a first-class ticket."

"That doesn't matter. I tell you, you must go to the van compartment."

"I tell you, I was permitted to travel in this compartment at Durban, and I insist on going on in it."

"No you won't. You must leave the compartment, or else I shall have to call a police constable to push you out."

"Yes, you may. I refuse to get out voluntarily."

When the constable arrived, Gandhi and his luggage were put off the train. He spent the night in a cold waiting room. (His experience is similar to that of Frederick Douglass being put off trains in New England.)

Gandhi was in turmoil that night. Should he return to India? Finish his work in South Africa? He wrote in his *Autobiography*: "The hardship to which I was subjected was superficial—only a symptom of the deep disease of color prejudice. I should try, if possible, to root out the disease and suffer hardships in the process."

The next day he protested to the general manager of the railway company who responded by justifying the conduct of the employees but also promised that Gandhi's first-class ticket would be honored through the rest of his trip. Gandhi had no trouble in claiming his first-class accommodations on the night train that evening, but at Charlestown he had to depart the train to take a stagecoach to Johannesburg. The white man in charge of the coach, called the "leader," did not want a coolie riding inside and ordered Gandhi to take a seat on the side of the coachbox while he rode inside. Gandhi accepted the injustice because he needed to complete his journey. Later that night, at a stop, the "leader" decided he wanted to smoke and take fresh air. He put a dirty sack on the footboard and called out, "Sami, you sit on this. I want to sit near the driver."

Gandhi refused to accept the insult, and with considerable fear he responded: "It was you who seated me here, though I should have been accommodated inside. I put up with the insult. Now that you want to sit outside and smoke, you would have me sit at your feet. I will not do so, but I am prepared to sit inside."

The enraged "leader" grabbed Gandhi's arm and tried to pull him from the coach. Gandhi held on to the brass rail and was determined not to let go. The "leader" was cursing and beating the coolie barrister.

The passengers observed what was happening and called out,

"Man, let him alone."

"Don't beat him."

"He is not to blame."

"He is right. If he can't stay there, let him come and sit with us."

The "leader" relented, but Gandhi was quickly learning that because of his color in the racist society of South Africa, he was not an English gentleman and never could be. When he arrived in Johannesburg, he was told that Indian merchants were prosperous and had learned to accept insults. Fellow Indians assured him, "This country is not for men like you."

In segregated South Africa, Gandhi continued to learn of the difficult conditions under which Indians lived. Wary of the success of Indian merchants and former indentured servants who became small farmers, the legislatures began to pass laws similar to the restrictive laws in the American slave states before the Civil War and after Radical Reconstruction. Traders were forced out. Indians coming into the Boer republic of the Transvaal had to pay a poll tax. Indians who were allowed to live in the Transvaal had to serve as waiters or as menial laborers. Indians could not walk on footpaths. Without a pass, they could not be out at night after 9 p.m. The provincial legislatures added more and more restrictions to discourage Indians from settling.

In May 1894, his difficult lawsuit successfully settled, Gandhi prepared to return to India. In the course of a farewell party, Gandhi saw in a Durban newspaper that the Natal legislative assembly was considering a bill to keep Indians from voting for representatives to the assembly. Gandhi remarked to a merchant at the party, "This bill, if it passes into law, will make our lot extremely difficult. It is the first nail into our coffin. It strikes at the root of our self-respect." He decided to stay on an extra month to organize protests against it.

Gandhi's shyness had disappeared in his year in South Africa. He had shown his willingness to stand up against authorities who mistreated him, and his skills as a writer and speaker had improved markedly.

He now made vigorous plans to oppose the proposed legislation. He established the Natal Indian Congress and organized a petition drive against the restrictive ordinance. The bill was passed, but the Congress collected ten thousand signatures

on a petition of protest sent to Lord Ripon, secretary of state
for the colonies. Gandhi made certain that the press in South
Africa and in Britain received stories about the abolition of the
Indians' right to vote. Eventually a compromise was reached:
Indians not on the voting rolls could not register, but those al-
ready enrolled could vote.

Gandhi had managed a small victory, but Indians remained
in danger of persecution. He would stay and continue to fight,
he said, if the merchants would guarantee his retainer fees
each year. Now his law practice and his earnings developed
rapidly as Gandhi argued against discrimination in the courts
and in the press through interviews and letters to the editor.

An indication of his growing social consciousness was the
founding in 1903 of a weekly newspaper, *Indian Opinion*,
which kept Indians and their supporters informed about problems in the Indian community. He put most of his savings into
the publication, whose offices were located on property that
Gandhi had bought fourteen miles from Durban—a communal settlement called Phoenix Farm. Life at the farm was simple, the prototype of many later ashrams (secluded religious
communities) founded by Gandhi.

Gandhi lived at Phoenix Farm at times, but he also resided
in Johannesburg where he had a lucrative law practice. He began to draw around him a group of supporters: Henry Polak, an
English-born newspaperman; Hermann Kallenbach, a German-
born architect; and Sonja Schlesin, of Russian origin—all three
Jewish; Albert West, manager of a printing press; and Reverend
Joseph Doke, a Baptist minister.

After the Zulu "rebellion" broke out in 1906, Gandhi organized the Indian Ambulance Corps to attend to Zulus,
whom the Europeans would not care for. The Zulus whom the
corps nursed had not been wounded in battle; some had been
shot by mistake, others "had been taken prisoners as sus-

pects," and had been mistreated. Gandhi was fully aware of the atrocities being committed: "This was no war but a manhunt, not only in my opinion, but also in that of many Englishmen with whom I had occasion to talk. To hear every morning reports of the soldiers' rifles exploding like crackers in innocent hamlets, and to live in the midst of them was a trial." Blacks and Indians alike in South Africa received brutal treatment, but Gandhi's work with the Ambulance Corps was a comprehensive humanitarian effort.

European leaders in South Africa were now speaking more ominously about Indians in that country. The Boer general Jan Christiaan Smuts said in October 1906, "The Asiatic cancer, which has eaten so deeply into the vitals of South Africa, ought to be resolutely eradicated." General Louis Botha, premier of the Transvaal from 1907 to 1910, declared, "If my party is returned to office we will undertake to drive the coolies out of the country within four years."

Gandhi learned from the draft ordinance published in the Transvaal *Gazette Extraordinary* of August 22, 1906, that all Asiatics over eight years of age would be required to register. The registrar would note any distinguishing marks of identification and take fingerprints. Failure to register would be punished with fines, imprisonment, or deportation. Certificates were to be produced at the command of any police officer, and private homes could be entered. Although indentured Indians had earlier been forced to carry passes when they left the farms where they worked, the new regulations applied to all free Indians as well. Fingerprinting, Gandhi believed, carried with it the stigma of criminality.

Believing that Indians were innocent of any wrongdoing in the Transvaal, Gandhi called for them to present a united front of resistance to the proposed law, referred to as the "Black Act," and he arranged a meeting to discuss the proposed ordinance.

At Johannesburg's Empire Theatre on September 11, 1906, three thousand attended a meeting organized by Gandhi to discuss the proposed ordinance. He explained to the large crowd the terms of the proposed law, and resolutions were drawn up calling for noncompliance. One of the speakers was Sheth Haji Habib, who requested that the resolution be passed "with God as witness."

Gandhi recognized the seriousness of such a vow, and in a closely argued speech he said, "We all believe in one and the same God, the differences of nomenclature in Hinduism and Islam notwithstanding." He argued that taking an oath of disobedience to a law, "with God as witness" could not be made lightly. In his speech he set forth some classic tenets of civil disobedience: "We might have to go to jail, where we might be insulted. We might have to go hungry and suffer extreme heat or cold. Hard labor might be imposed upon us. We might be flogged by rude warders. We might be fined heavily and our property might be attached and held up to auction if there are only a few resisters left." He also assumed that, as a matter of conscience, large numbers would join the movement. Gandhi would not read Thoreau's "Civil Disobedience" until the next year, but circumstances had forced him to envision a nonviolent way of refusing to obey an unjust law.

All in attendance took the oath that they would not submit to the ordinance should it become law. Gandhi, even then intent on influencing public opinion and appealing to British officials for help, now traveled to London to explain to responsible officials the tense anti-Asian problems in South Africa. Although Lord Elgin, secretary of state for the colonies, made no outright promises to Gandhi to disallow the ordinance, he did advise such action after Gandhi had left England to return to South Africa. But while Elgin let it be known that the British government would not permit such a law, in fact the Transvaal, which became a crown colony after the Boer War, would lose that status on January 1, 1907, and it could legislate as it desired after that date. Gandhi rightly considered Elgin's policy a trick.

The newly organized government of the Transvaal passed the Asiatic Registration Act in March 1907. The Black Act was to take effect July 31, and registration offices were opened July 1, 1907. Indians picketed these offices, passing out handbills and attempting to learn the names of those who registered in order to bring public pressure against them. Gandhi believed that not a single Indian felt it proper to submit to the law, but some complied because they were unwilling to accept jail time and the loss of goods or property that would result from non-compliance. Some leading Indian merchants arranged for permit officers to come to their homes so that they might register secretly. Alert Indian resisters generally learned of the merchants' actions, and pickets were placed in front of their stores.

Of thirteen thousand Indians in the Transvaal, only about five hundred registered. Gandhi kept the public informed about the struggle through articles in *Indian Opinion* and letters and interviews in other papers. At first he called the protest "passive resistance," but in a letter to the *Rand Daily Mail* he said that it "is not a resistance but a policy of communal suffering" (a concept Dr. King would later embrace). He became dissatisfied with the term "passive resistance," for the resistance was more active than passive.

For several weeks after the deadline, the Transvaal government refrained from making mass arrests of those who failed to register. Gandhi continued to advise Indians not to accept the registration ordinance because it took away "every vestige of manliness from Indians." In a statement that rings with the idealism of Ralph Waldo Emerson, he entreated his fellow Indians "to submit to a higher law, namely, that *which dictates* to mankind an idea of self-respect. . . ." Gandhi knew of Emerson's essay "The Oversoul"; *Indian Opinion* printed an extract from it on February 18, 1905. He may not have been the one at the paper to make the extract, but he surely read it. His interest in Emerson continued. From jail he wrote his son Manilal on March 25, 1909: "The [Emerson] essays to my mind contain the teaching of Indian wisdom in a western guru. It is interesting to see our own sometimes thus differently fashioned."

Thoreau came to Gandhi's attention in the early days of the noncooperation movement. On September 7, 1907, *Indian Opinion* carried an article titled "On the Duty of Civil Disobedience." The Archbishop of Canterbury had requested that the clergy not celebrate marriage between a husband and a deceased wife's sister, even though such marriages were permitted by English law. Gandhi argued in the article that passive resistance was the proper course of action for the law-abiding who sought redress from unjust laws. Thoreau was referred to as an authority: "Thoreau has said that we should be men before we are subjects and that there is no obligation imposed upon us by our consciences to give blind submission to any law, no matter what force or majority backs it."

Years later Gandhi wrote Henry S. Salt, Thoreau's biographer, that he first read Thoreau "when I was in the thick of [the] passive resistance struggle." He remembered that a friend, probably Polak, had sent him the "Civil Disobedience" essay and that it had "left a deep impression" upon him. Gandhi went on, "I translated a portion for the readers of *Indian Opinion* in South Africa which I was then editing, and I made copious extracts for the English part of that paper."

Thoreau's essay seemed "so convincing and truthful that I felt the need of knowing more of Thoreau, and I came across your life of him, his 'Walden,' and other short essays, all of which I read with great pleasure and equal profit." It is not certain just when Gandhi read these additional works by and about Thoreau, but it was probably late in 1907. Gandhi was not hesitant in speaking about Thoreau's influence on him. In 1931 he told the American reporter Webb Miller that he "took the name of my movement from Thoreau's essay." Until he read Thoreau's "Civil Disobedience," he said, he had not found a suitable translation for the Indian word *Satyagraha*.

Gandhi's introductory paragraph on Thoreau and the extracts from "Civil Disobedience" appeared in the Gujarati language in *Indian Opinion* on September 7, 1907, under the title "Duty of Disobeying Laws." Gandhi wrote:

"Many years ago, there lived in America a great man named Henry David Thoreau. His writings are read and pondered over by millions of people. Some of them put his ideas into practice. Much importance is attached to his writings because Thoreau himself was a man who practiced what he preached. Impelled by a sense of duty, he wrote much against his own country, America. He considered it a great sin that the Americans held many persons in the bonds of slavery. He did not rest content with saying this, but took all other necessary steps to put a stop to this trade. One of those steps consisted in not paying any taxes to the State in which the slave trade was being carried on. He was imprisoned when he stopped paying the taxes due from him. The thoughts which occurred to him during his imprisonment were boldly original and were published in the form of a book. The title of this article conveys the general sense of the English title of his book. . . . Both his example and writings are at present exactly applicable to the Indians in the Transvaal." The important message to Indian readers was that unfair and unjust laws should be resisted.

Gandhi then prepared in English another introduction about Thoreau to accompany excerpts from "Civil Disobedience." The article appeared under the title "For Passive Resisters" in *Indian Opinion* on October 26, 1907. The tone and content of the introduction are somewhat different from the one earlier published in Gujarati. In the intervening weeks Gandhi had probably done more reading and thinking about Thoreau. The English article begins with a quotation from Tolstoy: "The principle of State necessity can bind only those men to disobey God's law who, for the sake of worldly advantages, try to reconcile the irreconcilable; but a Christian, who sincerely believes that the fulfillment of Jesus' teaching shall bring him salvation, cannot attach any importance to this principle." Gandhi apparently had read Tolstoy's *The Kingdom of God Is Within You* during his first year in South Africa when he made an extensive study of religions. Tolstoy's work, with its literal application of the Sermon on the Mount, made a lasting impression on him.

Gandhi then offers a clear indication of how important Thoreau's essay was to him and the entire movement then in its early stages: "David Thoreau was a great writer, philosopher, poet, and withal a most practical man, that is, he taught nothing he was not prepared to practice in himself. He was one of the greatest and most moral men America has produced. At the time of the abolition of slavery movement, he wrote his famous essay 'On the Duty of Civil Disobedience.' He went to gaol for the sake of his principles and suffering humanity. His essay has, therefore, been sanctified by suffering. Moreover, it is written for all time. Its incisive logic is unanswerable. During the last week of October—a month of sore temptation to Asiatic passive resisters, whose silent suffering has now reached the whole civilized world—we present the following extracts from Thoreau's essay. . . ."

The extracts from Thoreau's essay, in both English and Gujarati versions, emphasize the right of the minority to ignore unjust laws and the moral justification for choosing to disobey those laws, accepting the consequences, and being sent to prison. Gandhi's movement was in its early stages when he read "Civil Disobedience." Indians had not yet begun breaking the law and going to jail. Thoreau's essay did not give him the original idea for opposing the Black Act, but it provided important support for him as the movement expanded.

When Gandhi accepted ideas from the great thinkers, he believed in putting them into practice. Jesus, Tolstoy, Thoreau, and Socrates all confirmed that civil disobedience by whatever name—passive resistance or *Satyagraha*—was the correct way to confront unjust laws.

In November 1907, *Indian Opinion* also published an article on "Socrates as Passive Resister." Socrates was interpreted as a man of principle who followed his conscience and made no attempt to escape the consequences of his disobedience: "For him, when there was a choice between his conscience—what he knew to be good—and what the government of the day had ordered, and what he knew to be wrong, there was no hesitation even though it might have cost him his life."

Readers of *Indian Opinion* were not allowed to forget Thoreau's essay, and the paper soon announced a prize of ten guineas for an essay on "The Ethics of Passive Resistance." The terms of the contest made it clear that the editors believed that passive resistance was "a fulfillment of Jesus' famous saying, 'Resist not evil,'" and that entries should deal with Thoreau's essay, Tolstoy's *The Kingdom of God Is Within You*, the Apology of Socrates, and other appropriate religious references.

On December 28, 1907, Gandhi was arrested and called before the magistrate to show why, having failed to register, he should not be deported from the Transvaal. He ignored the order and was sentenced to two months of simple imprisonment, though he requested the maximum sentence. He remembered a "slight feeling of awkwardness due to the fact that I was standing as an accused in the very Court where I had often appeared as counsel." He added: "But I well remember that I considered the former role as far more honorable than the latter, and did not feel the slightest hesitation in entering the prisoner's box."

In jail, Gandhi was soon joined by seventy-six Indians who had also courted detention. He found that there were two classes of convicts, whites and blacks. Asians were placed in the black wards. As his sentence was one of simple imprisonment, Gandhi had ample time for study and made use of the prison library, borrowing the works of Carlyle and the Bible. Chinese residents of the Transvaal had also declared civil disobedience because of the anti-Asian laws, and from one of them he borrowed the *Qur'an-i-sharif* translated into English. He read the speeches of Thomas Huxley, and the essays of Bacon. He had with him an annotated edition of the *Gita*, and he read it in the mornings. At noon he read the Koran, and at night he taught the Bible to Mr. Foretoon, a Chinese Christian, who wished to learn English.

Gandhi's interpretation of the *Gita* is helpful in understanding his concepts of civil disobedience that justified his going to jail. Since his days in London when he first read the *Gita*, he had refused the fundamentalist interpretation that it was an historical work justifying violence. He believed that "under the guise of physical warfare, it described the duel that perpetually went on in the hearts of mankind, and the physical warfare was brought in merely to make the descriptions of the internal duel more alluring." In *A Week on the Concord and Merrimack Rivers*, Thoreau had protested the seeming justification of violence in the *Gita*, though he did not write an extended criticism of it as Gandhi did in *The Gita According to Gandhi*. Gandhi would have learned of Thoreau's interest in Hindu religious thought from Salt's biography of Thoreau and from his reading of *Walden*.

Gandhi insisted that those who studied the *Mahabharata*, of which the *Gita* was a part, would conclude that the "victors shed tears of sorrow and repentance," and that the second chapter of the *Gita*, rather than teaching the rules of warfare, demonstrated how man could achieve perfection. He accepted the Urdu saying, "Adam is not God, but he is a spark of the Divine." Gandhi could find in the works of Emerson this same idea of the spark of divinity in mankind, and Gandhi believed that all persons had a portion of divinity within themselves. He took the next step: people should endeavor to form a nexus with God as abstract Truth. If Truth led Gandhi to disobey the unjust law, he would as a follower of Truth declare nonviolent civil disobedience and go to jail.

The supreme ethical concept that would lead to God, Gandhi believed, was the renunciation of the fruits of action. By this interpretation of the *Gita*, Gandhi was a believer in taking action, but he would renounce all honors, riches, special favors, and titles resulting from such action. That is why he had concerns about the title conferred upon him by the millions— Mahatma (Great Soul). He wanted his efforts to benefit humanity, not bestow on him a title.

On January 30, 1908, Gandhi was taken from jail to Pretoria to meet with General Smuts, who proposed that Indians register voluntarily, under no compulsion of law, in which case the Black Law would be repealed. Gandhi had said earlier that compulsion, not the fingerprinting itself, was the major problem with the Black Act.

Gandhi signed the agreement and was released from prison that day. When he reached Johannesburg he called a meeting to explain the settlement. While most Indians were willing to accept the compromise, a rumor began to circulate that Gandhi had betrayed the Indians for a bribe of fifteen thousand pounds sterling. When Gandhi went to the Asian office to register, he was brutally beaten by a man who believed that rumor. He was then carried to the home of the white Baptist minister J. J. Doke for recuperation.

After six thousand Indians in the Transvaal voluntarily registered by the deadline of May 9, 1908, General Smuts declared that he had made no agreement with Gandhi and refused to support the repeal of compulsory registration. Clearly Gandhi had placed too much trust in Smuts. Indians now decided to burn their certificates unless the Black Act was rescinded. It was not. On the afternoon of August 16, 1908, on the grounds of the Hamidia Mosque in Johannesburg, about two thousand certificates were placed in a huge cauldron, doused with kerosene, and set afire. The man who had assaulted Gandhi was present and announced that he was wrong to have caused him bodily harm. He too burned his certificate. Gandhi assured the man that he had never felt any resentment against him. Gandhi had turned the other cheek, as he was to do many times in the years ahead.

We do not know to what extent the dramatic burning of the certificates was an inevitable result of General Smuts's betrayal, or how much the action owed to a belief in the cleansing qualities of fire, or whether or not it was influenced by William Lloyd Garrison's burning of the U.S. Constitution on

July 4, 1854, because that document legitimized slavery. Thoreau was present during that act of civil disobedience, and he gave "Slavery in Massachusetts" as a lecture at the meeting. Gandhi would have read about Garrison's dramatic action in Salt's biography of Thoreau. (Later, *Indian Opinion* printed excerpts from Garrison's writings.)

The correspondent for the London *Daily Mail*, describing the burning of the registration certificates in Johannesburg, compared the event to the American colonists' Boston Tea Party. "I do not think," Gandhi mused in *Satyagraha in South Africa*, that "this comparison did more than justice to the Indians seeing . . . the whole might of the British Empire was ranged against hundreds of thousands . . . in America [and] in South Africa a helpless body of 13,000 Indians had challenged the . . . Government of the Transvaal."

After the Transvaal government began to arrest those Indians who had burned their certificates, many were heavily fined or deported to India. Gandhi was arrested and sentenced to the Volksrust prison on October 10, 1908. Hoping to discourage civil disobedience, the government began to impose hard labor on the prisoners. At seven each morning Gandhi and other prisoners began digging with a shovel. Most of Gandhi's compatriots were not accustomed to hard physical labor. Gandhi's own hands were covered with blisters. One of his fellow workers fainted, and for a time Gandhi began to wonder if he had misled the resisters who followed him to jail. But he decided that he had, after all, given the only advice possible under totally unacceptable circumstances.

Although Gandhi worked all day, he had time to read in the early morning, in the evenings, and on holidays. He read Ruskin, the essays of Thoreau, parts of the Bible, and several books in Gujarati. As they had done before, the writings of

Ruskin and Thoreau provided him "arguments in favor of our fight."

He ended his account of his second stay in prison by quoting Thoreau's passage from "Civil Disobedience": "I saw that, if there was a wall of stone between me and my townsmen, there was a still more difficult one to climb or break before they could get to be as free as I was."

In two months Gandhi was released from prison, but he continued his civil disobedience campaign and was sentenced again for three months of hard labor in February 1909. This time he was surrounded by hardened criminals, one who had attempted murder, one who had been convicted of bestiality, and two others who had been convicted of sodomy. Gandhi was placed in solitary confinement. His cell was poorly ventilated and lighted, and he was assigned jobs that caused him great physical discomfort. General Smuts was apparently trying to break his spirit. Again Gandhi read in prison: Carlyle's *French Revolution*, Tolstoy, Emerson, the Upanishads. This was his most difficult prison time thus far, but his spirit was not broken.

Gandhi's movement had reached an impasse. Of 13,000 Indians in the Transvaal, 2,500 had served time in prison for civil disobedience, and 6,000 had fled the province. Gandhi needed to win British support or the movement would fail. The British Indian Association decided to make yet another appeal to London, and Gandhi and Haji Habib were sent to try to persuade the British to change the hated Asiatic laws. Lord Ampthill, former governor of Madras and acting viceroy of India, and a friend of Gandhi's, advised him to negotiate behind the scenes, not to make public speeches or give interviews to the press. Gandhi met other prominent British leaders to give them details of the problems faced by Indians in the

Transvaal, and while many of his listeners seemed sympathetic, nothing positive resulted. Smuts was also in London at the time, and whatever he was told privately about the Indian situation did not change his mind, though he did make enigmatic statements. Gandhi was still learning how to use civil disobedience effectively, and private negotiations proved unsuccessful. Appeal to a wide public was needed, as Gandhi learned painfully.

Gandhi still felt the need for validation of his strategy of civil disobedience. In their writings, Thoreau, Ruskin, and Tolstoy had provided him with assurances of the rightness of his course. He needed a personal touch too, but Thoreau and Ruskin were dead. The elderly Tolstoy was still alive and was regarded by many as one of the world's great writers. In his late years he had turned to writing religious and moral tracts that displayed his contempt for modern civilization and its governments. He favored manual labor and rejected private property. He opposed the use of violence and preached suffering without offering resistance to the acts of evil. On October 1, 1909, Gandhi wrote a long letter to Tolstoy, in which he carefully presented the Indian case.

Tolstoy responded on October 9, expressing his pleasure in receiving Gandhi's letter: "May God help all our dear brothers and co-workers in the Transvaal. This fight between gentleness and brutality, between humility and love on one side, and conceit and violence on the other, makes itself ever more strongly felt to us also—especially in the sharp conflicts between religious obligations and the laws of the State—expressed by the conscientious objection to render military service."

The Gandhi-Tolstoy correspondence continued after Gandhi returned to South Africa from his failed trip to London. Tolstoy's last letter to Gandhi, on September 7, 1910,

was a long meditation on civil disobedience, completely vali-
dating what Gandhi was attempting to do in South Africa. Un-
officially Tolstoy was appointing Gandhi his successor in
passive resistance work.

At this period of his life Gandhi had formulated a "Confession of Faith, 1909" from a variety of sources: Indian history and mythology, and ideas from Tolstoy, Ruskin, and
Thoreau. He now seemed opposed to modern civilization altogether: "The railways, telegraphs, hospitals, lawyers, doc-
tors, and such like have all to go. . . ." He called for a return
to the "simple peasant life," and urged that Indians give up
wearing machine-made clothing.

In late May 1910 the wealthy Hermann Kallenbach purchased eleven hundred acres of land about twenty miles from
Johannesburg and allowed Gandhi to use it for the *Satyagraha*
struggle. Phoenix Farm was far away, and a cooperative venture
was needed near the primary seat of the protest. Gandhi named
this new site Tolstoy Farm. The land was fertile with already
producing fruit trees, and was now developed as a commune for
resisters and their families. Food and housing were simple, and
everyone was expected to do manual labor. Gandhi worked relentlessly to make Tolstoy Farm a success. He supervised all its
activities and still managed to attend to his law practice in Johannesburg. He often walked the twenty-one miles to his office
and then walked home after completing his work for the day.

Gandhi focused much of his formidable energy into making
Tolstoy Farm a success. He continued to work with *Indian
Opinion* and reduced his law practice. Still, the South African
government seemed to be ignoring the Indian question. All that
changed in March 1913 when a Supreme Court decision inval-
idated all marriages not celebrated according to Christian rites.

Indians immediately decided that mass civil disobedience must be used against this new governmental edict. The first group to court arrest were women from Phoenix Farm. They crossed into the Transvaal without permit and were arrested. Mrs. Gandhi was sentenced to three months at hard labor. Another group of women crossed into Natal, and they too were arrested.

At the coal mining town of Newcastle, indentured Indian miners began to recount the injustices they suffered, and decided to strike. Thousands refused to work, and they were locked in their quarters. Gandhi rushed to Newcastle to direct the protest. He decided to lead a large band of strikers on a thirty-six-mile, two-day march to the Transvaal border, cross, and thereby be subject to arrest. The goal was to fill the jails.

For the first time Gandhi organized a massive movement, providing food, water, and shelter to the protesters. He had to maintain discipline and convince the marchers that they must remain nonviolent and not resist arrest. Gandhi told the mine owners and the government that discriminatory acts against Indians had to be revoked before the march would be called off. There was no response.

More that two thousand people took part in the march, entering the Transvaal at Volksrust. As they proceeded, Gandhi was arrested, freed, then rearrested. Miners were arrested and sent back to the mines. The Transvaal was in turmoil. Gandhi, Polak, and Kallenbach were sentenced to prison, but with the news of Gandhi's arrest, twenty thousand workers in Natal went out on strike.

The government could not keep thousands in jail. A compromise was sought, and a commission was established to study the problem. Gandhi was released from jail in December

Gandhi led a march of more than two thousand protesters in the Transvaal after the South African government sought to invalidate Indian marriages. *(Peter Ruhe / GandhiServe)*

1913. He boycotted the commission because Indians were not represented, and with a vow of self-suffering, he adopted the dress of laborers. (Later in India, he refined his attire even more and wore homespun loin cloths, his legs and chest bare, his upper body covered only with a shawl in cold weather.)

Although Gandhi did not attend the commission meetings, he did send a letter stating Indian demands including the legalization of Hindu and Muslim marriages. The commission recommended compliance with these demands and in 1914 the Indian Relief Bill was passed.

With many of his goals achieved in South Africa, and with civil disobedience established as a successful and peaceful means of redressing grievances, Gandhi prepared to return to India. There, in his ensuing campaign of more than three decades to win independence for India from the British, the

By age forty-five, Gandhi had reverted to wearing homespun cloth. *(Vithalbhai Jhaveri / GandhiServe)*

strategy of civil disobedience predominated with only minor variations.

Upon his return to India in 1914, Gandhi spent months traveling, talking, and studying the enormous problems in his country. He investigated the plight of indigo growers in 1917. The next year he led a small civil disobedience campaign to benefit locked-out millworkers in Ahmedabad. In spite of the many problems in India, Gandhi could not at first identify an incident or major injustice that could be used to introduce a massive act of civil disobedience, by which he hoped, eventually, to bring home rule to his country. That changed in 1919 with the passage of the Rowlatt Act, an anti-sedition measure. According to this much-opposed law, those engaging in terrorist activities or suspected of doing so were to be tried in special courts, *in camera*, with no publication of the findings of the court. Those caught with seditious documents could be jailed for two years. Gandhi's pamphlets on *Unto This Last* and on Socrates were banned by the Raj (British rule). Speeches leading to breaches of the peace were forbidden.

Gandhi had found a cause he hoped would have widespread appeal, and he made a dramatic proposal: on April 6, 1919, all Indians were to go on strike for twenty-four hours. It was also to be a day of fasting to symbolize the humiliation they were enduring for the loss of many of their civil rights. But violence and rioting in many sections of the country forced Gandhi to call a halt to the action. Although this civil disobedience effort failed, it was clear that sand could be thrown into the machinery of government by those who did not wish to be misgoverned.

The Raj made a Himalayan blunder a few days later. General Dyer, in charge of the garrison in Amritsar, ordered that all public meetings were forbidden. Town criers were sent out to spread the word, but apparently they went to sparsely settled areas, and few people learned of the prohibition. On April 13, 1919, about 6,000 people assembled for a Sikh festival, not a protest meeting. An angered General Dyer ordered troops to fire into a crowd of Indians, killing 379 and wounding well over a thousand. Robert Payne in *The Life and Death of Mahatma Gandhi* concluded: "He wanted to inflict a salutary bloodletting that would be remembered for years to come." Dyer ordered that the wounded be left where they fell and their wounds not be tended to. But there was more. After a Miss Sherwood, headmistress of a school, had been attacked by a mob, General Dyer decreed that all Indians passing by where she was assaulted should crawl by. The soldiers interpreted this to mean that they should crawl on their bellies. Those who refused to follow orders were beaten. A whipping post was assembled, and Indians showing disrespect to Europeans were flogged. The general imposed a blackout of news reports, but his humiliation of Indians could be kept secret only briefly. Once the events became known, the stage was set for massive resistance to the Raj.

Over the next few years Gandhi organized high-profile mass movements, making certain that the press in India and throughout the world knew of civil disobedience protests. He became an international figure. His methods were admired and attacked: the personal beliefs he urged on his fellow Indians—spinning, wearing homespun garments, diet reform—were followed by millions but derided in much of the Western world. He was often arrested, and, as in South Africa, in prison he read and wrote newspaper articles, depositions, and his autobiography. He attempted self-purification through extended fasts—unto death at times—which placed the Raj in difficult situations. Gandhi's status was that of a holy man who was also a political leader of oppressed people, including "untouchables," the lower caste of Indians. He had millions of followers who hoped to gain freedom nonviolently.

Gandhi's program of civil disobedience (*Satyagraha*), influenced by Thoreau, was developed in a specific environment in South Africa and was then transferred to India before returning to the United States.

India won its independence on August 15, 1947, but the country was divided into India and Pakistan, a partition that Gandhi had tried valiantly to avoid. The partition was followed by dislocation, riots, and mass murder. Gandhi himself was assassinated by an extremist Hindu on January 30, 1948. He was widely praised as a man of peace who used nonviolent means to counter unjust laws and to win freedom for people under colonial rule. Long before Dr. King arrived on the scene, blacks recognized that the Gandhian method might be used in the United States.

VII

THE WALLS OF SEGREGATION
GO UP ONCE MORE

O take yer shoes from off yer feet,
Let my people go;
And walk into the golden street;
Let my people go.
—From "Go Down, Moses"

While the Ku Klux Klan of the Reconstruction South officially disbanded in 1869, local chapters remained and other white supremacy groups were organized. With white Southerners back in control after the end of Radical Reconstruction, blacks found their educational opportunities diminished and their voting rights damaged by poll taxes and unfair literacy tests—which uneducated Southern whites themselves could not pass, though of course they were allowed to vote. In 1869, Louisiana had 130,344 blacks registered to vote. After a new state constitution with discriminatory laws took effect, in 1900 only 5,320 blacks were registered to vote. The same disfranchisement occurred in all the former slaveholding states.

Blacks were forced into a segregated society. Schools, ho-
tels, barber shops, restaurants, trains, train stations, theaters,
water fountains, and public rest rooms were all segregated.
Local laws enforced these restrictions, and in 1896, in *Plessy
v. Ferguson*, the U.S. Supreme Court upheld the "separate but
equal" doctrine. As W. E. B. DuBois remarked, "The slave
went free, stood a brief moment in the sun, then moved back
again toward slavery." "Separate but equal" in practice became "separate and unequal." In former slave and former free
states, the stage was set again for civil disobedience.

In the South some disfranchised blacks attempted to register to vote but were refused on the basis of the biased literacy
test or the requirement of a poll tax. Refused, some of these
aspiring voters returned again the next year in a new effort to
register. Many of these civil disobedients then received visits
from the Klan-like white supremacy organizations. In former
free states, blacks generally were not restrained from voting.

White landowners in the South tried to keep blacks from
abandoning their sharecropping existence, often using local
law officials to enforce labor contract laws that would keep
blacks on the land. Blacks had great trouble using civil disobedience techniques to confront this difficulty because of
threats from Klan-like groups and law enforcement officials
who almost universally supported segregation policies and
were willing to enforce with violence those discriminatory
laws, codes, and conventions.

Although the police acted to maintain the color barrier on
public transportation, blacks continually objected to segregated seating on Southern streetcars. Between 1891 and 1910
there were organized protests in some twenty-five cities. In
some places, blacks walked instead of riding at the back of the
car. In some instances they bought buses and attempted to

establish their own transportation systems. These ventures failed from lack of funding and from stiff opposition by white authorities, but there was a growing sense that segregated public transportation might be vulnerable. Even some owners of the systems objected to the added expenses and controversy caused by forcing blacks to sit in segregated areas. There was much less segregation on public transportation in free states, but housing was segregated, as were many schools and churches throughout the country. Blacks faced enormous difficulties in job opportunities in all sections of the United States.

Lynchings were common in the South. Between 1889 and 1932, 3,745 people were lynched in the United States. Most of these were black men, but white men and black women were also killed. The usual charge was that a black man had raped a white woman, but black men who prospered were also in danger. Civil disobedience was dealt with harshly, as Darlene Clark Hine, William C. Hine, and Stanley Harrold illustrate in *The African-American Odyssey*: "In Valdosta, Georgia, in 1918 after Mary Turner's husband was lynched, she publicly vowed to bring those responsible to justice. Though she was eight months pregnant, a mob considered her determination a threat. They seized her, tied her ankles together, and hanged her upside down from a tree. A member of the mob slit her abdomen, and her nearly full-term child fell to the ground. The mob stomped the infant to death. They then set her clothes on fire and shot her." Fear certainly played a large part in maintaining segregation. The lynchings continued.

Booker T. Washington (1856–1915), founder and president of Tuskegee Institute in Alabama, was one of the most influential blacks of his time. He came to national attention with his Atlanta Exposition address in 1895, which demonstrated his optimism for black prospects at a time when an entire race was being suppressed. In that address he argued for education in the industrial and domestic arts instead of the liberal arts for black students. He accepted segregation and called for a peaceful coexistence of blacks and whites. These views were readily acceptable to the white power structure. Washington saw no need for civil disobedience.

Washington's views were opposed by Dr. W. E. B. DuBois (1868–1963), an intellectual who had received his Ph. D. from Harvard University. He opposed the limited educational opportunities advocated by Washington.

DuBois organized a 1905 meeting at Niagara Falls, New York, calling for the end of segregation, for better schools and housing, and for better job opportunities for blacks in all sections of the country. This radical group, called the Niagara Movement, had a brief existence, but it was willing to confront segregation policies, as Booker T. Washington was not.

After the early demise of the Niagara Movement, the National Association for the Advancement of Colored People (NAACP) was founded in 1909 by whites and blacks, including DuBois. Their aim was to renew "the struggle for civil and political liberty." DuBois became editor of the influential journal published by the organization, the *Crisis*, which by 1918 had a circulation of 100,000.

It was the *Crisis* that began to publish articles on the efforts of Gandhi to throw off colonial rule in India. In May 1921 the magazine noted that British rule was "opposed to the welfare of all the Indian people." In the July 1921 issue John Haynes Holmes, a white Unitarian minister, compared Gandhi to Jesus, a comparison often made in succeeding decades.

In August 1921 the *Crisis* republished Gandhi's open letter to all the British in India. Gandhi explained that for many years he had supported the British government, but after the Amritsar massacre, he had finally realized how oppressive that government was, and he would no longer defend its immorality.

Over a long period of time the *Crisis* published major articles about Gandhi and the civil disobedience (*Satyagraha*) movement. Not everyone agreed with Gandhi's methodology. E. Franklin Frazier, the African-American sociologist at Howard University, doubted that nonviolence would be enough to bring about major changes in the white suppression of blacks in the United States. He pointed out in the June 1924 issue, "Violent defense in local and specific instances has made white men hesitate to make wanton attacks upon Negroes. . . . But suppose there should arise a Gandhi to lead Negroes without hate in their hearts to stop tilling the fields of the South under the peonage system; to cease paying taxes to States that keep their children in ignorance; and to ignore the iniquitous disfranchisement and Jim-Crow laws. I fear we would witness an unprecedented massacre of defenseless black men and women in the name of Law and Order and there would scarcely be enough Christian sentiment in America to stay the flood of blood." Frazier could not envision what a Dr. King might accomplish, but he did understand that civil disobedience would be met with violence.

Black religious publications, black newspapers such as the *Chicago Defender*, and the mainstream press all published articles about the civil disobedience movement in India throughout the 1920s and '30s. Black publications were generally approving of the Gandhian movement, but mainstream papers most often published articles about Gandhi that were negative and biased toward British attitudes.

Growing racial unrest affected both the North and South in the early years of the twentieth century. Race riots occurred in Atlanta; Chicago; Springfield, Illinois; and Tulsa, Oklahoma, usually with widespread destruction. The Klan reappeared in

1915 after the release of D. W. Griffith's phenomenally popular *The Birth of a Nation*, based on Thomas Dixon's novel *The
Clansman*. In its rebirth, the Klan spread to Northern states
and fostered intolerance not only against blacks but also
against Jews and Catholics.

During World War I, 370,000 blacks were drafted, but all
branches of the military services were segregated. Mistreatment
of black servicemen was common. Housing in army bases was
inferior, and blacks in the navy were routinely assigned to duty
as cooks and waiters; whites often refused to salute black officers. Boom economic times during the war precipitated migra-
tions of civilian blacks from rural areas in the South to New
York, Chicago, and many other cities, where their lives were
only moderately improved. Churches were segregated in many
parts of the country. Schools were often segregated. The best
jobs were rarely open to them. The war over, black servicemen
returned to the same segregated society they had known before
the beginning of America's involvement in the war.

An early mass movement of American blacks was led by
Marcus Garvey (1887–1940). Born in Jamaica, Garvey emi-
grated to New York in 1916. He was an energetic organizer,
and his Universal Negro Improvement Association empha-
sized black pride and the greatness of blacks' African past. He
urged a "back to Africa" movement and appealed for the sol-
idarity of all people of color. At a Madison Square Garden
speech in August 1920, he declared, "India is striking out for
freedom; and the Negroes of the world shall do no less than
strike out also for freedom."

Garvey praised Gandhi: "For twenty-five years Gandhi has
been agitating the cause of his countrymen," he said in 1922,
and "The British people are now feeling the pressure of
Gandhi's propaganda. It is customary for them to suppress the

cause of liberty. It is customary of them to execute and imprison the leaders of the cause of liberty everywhere."

Although Garvey's newspaper, the *Negro World*, often mentioned Gandhi favorably, Garvey was primarily concerned with resettling blacks in Africa, not establishing a Gandhian civil disobedience movement in the United States. He raised money to fund a steamship line to transport United States blacks back to Africa, but the plan never came to fruition. He was convicted of misuse of funds and in 1925 sent to a federal penitentiary. In 1927 he was pardoned and deported to Jamaica. Without a dynamic leader, his organization in the United States declined and finally disappeared.

Although Garvey claimed to have 6 million followers in 1923, 500,000 is probably a more accurate figure. He did not appeal, as Franklin and Moss have written, to "the unlettered and inexperienced urban element, recently removed from the farm. . . ." Large numbers of Garvey's followers learned of the Gandhian movement from the *Negro World*.

As stories about Gandhi continued to appear, popular black interest grew in bringing a similar movement to the United States. Gordon Hancock, an NAACP leader, in March 1931, published an article titled "Wanted: A Black Reformer," arguing, "There must be a reformation within the Negro race! More and more we must turn our minds and hearts to spiritual values. In the last analysis there is more hope for the Negro in a loin-cloth with the spirit of a Gandhi than in a broadcloth with notions he has no way of satisfying."

Many of the articles about Gandhi in the twenties and thirties appeared in church publications, and they often referred to Gandhi as a "little, bare, brown skeleton of a man, not professing Christ, but living His teachings. . . ." The *Chicago Defender* in January 1932 advocated one of Gandhi's strategies: Do not pay taxes. Although the *Defender* did not make the Thoreau-Gandhi connection, it argued that if masses of African Americans would declare, "No I'll pay no taxes unless I can be a citizen; VOTE, hold office," they would begin to see change.

To provide more systematic information about Gandhi's methods, Richard B. Gregg, a white Quaker, published in 1935 an influential guide to the Indian leader's method in *The Power of Non-violence*. Gregg sent his first copies to DuBois, writing, "I believe it is more important for Negroes . . . to understand this new method of handling conflict than for any other groups of the population." Gregg believed that once nonviolent resistance "is understood and used in disciplined, organized mass fashion, there will be an end to tyranny and oppression of all kinds."

As Gandhi's followers began to appear in the United States to speak about the Mahatma and nonviolence, Quakers and other church groups began to send delegations to India to investigate the Gandhian movement. These were small but influential groups who appealed to members of black churches, pacifists such as Quakers, and radical students.

Benjamin E. Mays (1894 or 1895–1984), the prominent black who was the dean of the School of Religion at Howard University and later president of Morehouse College, interviewed Gandhi in India in 1936. Born in South Carolina to tenant farmers, Mays had struggled to receive a high school education and had then entered Bates College. After he earned his degree, he taught for a time before beginning graduate work at the University of Chicago, where he received a Ph.D. in 1935. He was a Baptist minister who believed in social change and an outspoken opponent of racial segregation.

In his autobiography, *Born to Rebel*, Mays recalled why he had wanted to meet Gandhi "who had done so much to make

Indians proud of their history and culture; who had identified himself with fifty million untouchables, determined to lift them to a place of dignity and respectability in the life of India; and who had started a movement for India's independence." Mays's ninety-minute interview with Gandhi took place at Gandhi's ashram at Wardha soon after Mays arrived in Bombay on Christmas eve. Gandhi spoke at length about the nature of nonviolence. Mays accepted the superiority of that strategy over violence but expressed his doubts about its application on a mass scale. Gandhi responded that civil disobedients had to be carefully trained and that with practice the method was effective.

No doubt thinking of blacks as a minority in white America, Mays asked, "How is a minority to act against an overpowering majority?"

Gandhi responded, "I would say that a minority can do much more in the way of non-violence than a majority. I had less diffidence in handling my minority in South Africa than I had here in handling a majority."

Upon his return to the United States, Mays wrote six perceptive articles about his Indian experiences for the *Norfolk Journal and Guide*. He argued that black people "have much to learn from the Indians. . . . They have learned how to sacrifice for a principle. They have learned how to sacrifice position, prestige, economic security and even life itself for what they consider a righteous and respectable cause. Thousands of them in recent times have gone to jail for their cause." It was two decades before blacks in the South acted on a massive scale to end segregation and seek their civil rights nonviolently. By that time Mays had moved to Morehouse College, where he was a mentor of Martin Luther King, Jr., who was to become the leader of the freedom movement in the United States.

A. Philip Randolph (1889–1979), the labor organizer and civil rights activist, came to national prominence when in 1937 he secured a union contract for the Brotherhood of Sleeping Car Porters, the first black union. This success gave him prestige among blacks and whites, and he was soon engaged in threatening a nonviolent, civil disobedience campaign.

Randolph became a national figure at a time when blacks continued to be excluded from most trade unions. In virtually all parts of the United States they went to segregated schools, lived in segregated housing, suffered major discrimination, and in many parts of the country were denied the right to vote. In the years between the two world wars, blacks in the South were unable to attend flagship state universities or any college not specifically established for them. They did enroll in major state universities outside the former slave states but were often badly treated. The University of Illinois at Urbana-Champaign, for example, was located in twin cities that still maintained many vestiges of segregation. Within the university itself, blacks were tolerated. A chapter of the Ku Klux Klan had been founded on the campus in 1906 and remained in existence there until 1925. Supposedly it was an all-white social club, but the student newspaper on January 9, 1923, reported that its members had been seen in hoods and gowns. University officials apparently did little to decertify the Klan on campus, nor did university officials attempt to desegregate restaurants, barber shops, and housing.

In the 1930s the Student Union on the University of Illinois campus presented minstrel shows, with whites blacking their faces with cork. In 1939 the university president declared that the humor in the shows was inappropriate, but the minstrels continued another year before being disbanded. The stage was set in Urbana-Champaign after World War II for a movement of civil disobedience to end the most flagrant examples of racial segregation on campus and in the cities.

As the United States began to rearm in 1940 and 1941, blacks found themselves virtually barred from jobs in the rapidly developing defense industries with their "whites only" policies, following national custom. White Americans were emerging from the hardships of the Great Depression, but blacks were still primarily confined to menial low-paying jobs. Franklin D. Roosevelt, elected to a third term in 1940, was reluctant to end discrimination for fear of offending his Southern supporters. A. Philip Randolph had a plan in December 1940 to force changes in discriminatory laws, and he had an idea how to do it: "I think we ought to get 10,000 Negroes and march down Pennsylvania Avenue asking for jobs in defense plants and integration of the armed forces. It would shake up Washington."

Randolph believed in the power of black people to bring about change; the examples of Gandhian mass movements were well known to him and to the black community. In the midst of planning for the march, he said, "Only the voice of the masses will be heard and heeded—Negro America has never spoken as a mass, an organized mass." He began organizing across the country, his goals clear, his message public. Roosevelt watched warily. He sent his wife, Eleanor, and Mayor Fiorello La Guardia of New York to see Randolph, asking that the march be called off in the national interest. Randolph refused. Roosevelt then partially capitulated. On June 25, 1941, he issued Executive Order #8802 which declared in part: "There shall be no discrimination in the employment of workers in the defense industry or government because of race, creed, color, or national origin." To make certain the directive was carried out, the administration established the Fair Employment Practices Committee.

Randolph called off the march, but he maintained a skeleton planning committee for such a march in the future as a
way of keeping pressure on the government. One of his demands was in fact not met: discrimination in the armed forces
was not forbidden. This inequity was not remedied until the
administration of Harry S Truman. Still, Randolph had considerable success by threatening a peaceful mass movement,
proving that he was willing to use some of Gandhi's techniques. By 1943 he had thought through the similarities and
differences between his movement and Gandhi's. He defined
the March on Washington Movement as "constitutional obedience or non-violent goodwill direct action." He recognized
that the Gandhians wanted to transfer government power
from the British to the Indian people. African Americans, Randolph argued, did not "desire to see the collapse of American
civil government," and they were "not seeking independence
as a racial unit." Randolph demonstrated his conservative approach, asserting that the March on Washington Movement
was not asking "the Negroes in the armed forces or defense industries to disobey commands or stop work at any time."

Bayard Rustin (1912–1987) came to prominence as a
Gandhian in the 1940s and often worked with Randolph.
Rustin was born in Pennsylvania, and—unusual for a black
man—he was a Quaker. Early in his adult life he toyed with
communism but soon abandoned that radical ideology. In the
1940s, working primarily through churches and college
groups, and at a time when the United States was preparing
for war and later was at war, Rustin traveled relentlessly
throughout the country spreading the word of Gandhian nonviolence. He was also a founder of the Congress of Racial
Equality, an organization dedicated to racial justice. Nonviolent resistance, Rustin said, was not "just a policy" but "a way

of life." He noted perceptively: "Non-violence will be a difficult message to give the Negro people." He recognized that a mass movement required discipline, something Gandhi was not able to achieve fully in the disparate Hindu and Muslim communities in India.

A conscientious objector, Rustin served time in federal prison during World War II. After the war he became still more widely known as he continued to urge nonviolence and racial equality, and as he worked closely with many of the most prominent civil rights leaders. He was not to become the American Gandhi, largely because he was known to be gay and had been arrested for homosexual activities. Most often he had to work behind the scenes in the developing civil rights movements.

With war industries, especially aircraft plants and shipyards, now open to blacks, there were mass movements of blacks to industrial cities. Discrimination in housing and schooling continued, but the cycle of subsistence farming in the South was broken. Of the two major labor unions, blacks did become members of the Congress of Industrial Organizations (CIO), but the American Federation of Labor (AFL) was not then open to black membership. The wall of discrimination in all branches of the military persisted, though there were a few cracks. Black pilots—the Tuskegee Airmen—were trained and served with distinction, as did black women who served as nurses.

Black Americans returning from service in the armed forces came home in 1945 to a country still segregated. Black veterans could take advantage of the GI Bill, but if they lived in the South they were confined to black colleges and universities. If they enrolled in Northern, Midwestern, and Western universities, they often faced discriminatory practices. The University of Illinois at Urbana-Champaign was not the best or worst in its treatment of blacks in the late forties and fifties. The small number of blacks enrolled in the years after the war felt they were "living behind enemy lines," but they succeeded "against all odds" in Urbana-Champaign and on campus.

Young black women, like the returning veterans, were often treated badly. One who was to have a distinguished career as an educator remembers that one of her Illinois professors returned all her papers and exams unmarked except for the grade of C. When she arranged to speak with the professor, he told her, "I am not reading anything you write. Negroes have only an average intelligence. Since you're an undergraduate, I'll give you Cs." She later recalled: "It did not bother me at all. Whatever the reasons, I had a positive enough self-concept that he was not big enough to destroy it. My immediate response was, 'You're an ignorant man,' and I made the vow to teach children to be intelligent and to think for themselves, and I will destroy everything he stood for."

Black students had to form close bonds to survive. Black fraternities and sororities "were our salvation," one Illinois survivor of the fifties reported. "It was like being inside the circled wagons. . . . We all had to bond because we went through so much hell just to exist, to get through school. People who didn't hang with us dropped out; they couldn't go to school and fight racism on their own, in terms of their mental health. A lot of people did go home. Those who stayed got close. The fraternities and sororities—they kept us sane."

One of the first black athletes to receive a full scholarship to play basketball had better experiences. He felt no discrimination from coaches or fellow players on campus, but when the Illinois team played a game in Kentucky, the story was different: "The fans called me the 'n' word and 'black boy.' We lost by one point. . . . I remember I took the last shot of the game and missed. Coming off the court, one guy said to me, 'Good thing you missed it, boy; we'd've had to cut your ears off and send them to your parents."

While discrimination on the University of Illinois campus was not then met with civil disobedience protests, that was not true off campus. Some barber shops in Urbana-Champaign had signs, "We Don't Cut Hair of Dogs or Niggers." After protests, these signs came down, but when a black person came into the shop, it was "just closing" and he was denied service. Some of the students planned a nonviolent campaign against the barbers. One of the organizers recalled, "We sent someone to every shop with annoying regularity. We hit them in the pocketbook and interrupted their flow of business." Within a month the barbers gave in and quit closing as soon as a black man came through the door.

Segregation was much worse in Anniston, Alabama; Americus, Georgia; Chesterfield, South Carolina; Monroe, North Carolina; Jackson, Mississippi; Commerce, Texas. In the first decade after World War II, segregation continued in these cities and elsewhere in the South as a way of life.

Through its Legal Defense and Educational Fund, the NAACP began to win legal victories against institutional racism. In 1944 the Supreme Court declared "white primaries"— in which blacks were not allowed to vote to nominate candidates for public office—unconstitutional. In 1950 the Court ruled that a black law student at the University of Texas at Austin should attend classes with the white students. The university had previously set up a separate (and clearly unequal) program to keep him segregated from white students.

The NAACP victories, though isolated, were important, but they barely cracked the country's massively segregated systems.

In 1954 the Supreme Court's ruling in *Brown v. Board of Education* began the process of changing the system. Chief Justice Warren delivered this opinion: "We conclude that in the field of public education the doctrine of 'separate but equal' has no place. Separate educational facilities are inherently unequal. Therefore, we hold that the plaintiffs and others similarly situated for whom the actions have been brought are, by reason of the segregation complained of, deprived of the equal protection of the laws guaranteed by the Fourteenth Amendment."

The long-run importance of this ruling is forcefully stated in *The African-American Odyssey*: "The *Brown* decision would eventually lead to the dismantling of the entire structure of Jim Crow laws that regulated important aspects of black life in America: movement, work, marriage, education, housing, even death and burial. The *Brown* decision, more than any other case, signaled the emerging primacy of equality as a guide to constitutional decisions." "Eventually" is a key word here, for early on the Court's ruling was largely ignored or rejected. In the following year the Supreme Court, in a decision now known as *Brown II*, called for desegregation in the schools to proceed with "all deliberate speed"—interpreted in most districts as "no speed." A massive disobedience campaign by whites, often in the form of White Citizens Councils, began. Private academies were established to keep blacks from attending school with white children. A defiant judge in Mississippi wrote that the Court "shall not make us drink from this cup." Reflecting Southern racism, he wrote, "When law transgresses the moral and ethical sanctions and standards of the mores, invariably strife, bloodshed and revolution follow in the wake of its attempted enforcement." For many years the executive and legislative branches of the federal government did little to make certain that schools were desegregated.

The black community grew disappointed and angered that the promise of *Brown v. Board of Education* was mostly abrogated. The consequence was rising tension over segregation in all its aspects. In 1955 the murder of Emmett Till, a young black man of fourteen from Chicago who was visiting in Mississippi, inflamed all those who were disgusted with continued lynchings in the country. Till had supposedly said, "Bye, baby" to the wife of the owner of a store where he had made a purchase. Southern womanhood had been violated. Till was kidnapped, tortured, and killed. Two arrests were made, and although Till's uncle gave explicit testimony about the kidnappers, the two were found not guilty and later bragged in a national magazine article that they had done the deed. Till's mother insisted on an open-casket funeral so that it could be obvious to blacks and whites alike that the young man had been tortured and murdered. In white society there was growing embarrassment over the gross injustice of vigilante lynchings and the obvious anti-democratic quality of segregation. It was time for a Thoreau-Gandhi crusader.

CHAPTER

VIII

"TRUMPETS BEGIN TO SOUND": MARTIN LUTHER KING, JR., AND THE BEGINNINGS OF THE CIVIL DISOBEDIENCE MOVEMENT

Up de walls of Jericho,
He marched with spear in hand;
"Go blow dem ram horns," Joshua cried,
"Kase de battle am in my hand."
Den de lamb ram sheep horns begin to blow,
Trumpets begin to sound,
Joshua commanded de chillen to shout,
An de walls come tumbling down.
—From "Joshua Fit de Battle of Jericho"

❦ Another Thoreau who went to jail as a matter of principle in the fight against slavery? Another Gandhi leading a nonviolent civil disobedience campaign? Another Moses leading
oppressed people to freedom? Could such a person or persons
arise in the black community in the middle of the twentieth
century?

That leader—those leaders—began to emerge after December 1, 1955, in Montgomery, Alabama. On that day Rosa Parks, a demure, religious, forty-two-year-old seamstress, entered a bus after 5 P.M. at Court Square. She had spent a working day at a local department store. She paid her ten-cent fare and took a seat in the middle section of the bus that was considered racially neutral, subject to claim by the driver if a white person were standing.

Blacks made up about 70 percent of the patronage of the Montgomery bus system, but they were routinely mistreated and humiliated. Some entered the bus, paid the fare, and were then forced to depart by the front door and reenter through the back door. All too often the bus driver had deliberately pulled away before they could make it to the back door. Black passengers were frequently cursed and demeaned, called "niggers," "apes," and "black cows."

When Rosa Parks's bus stopped in front of the Empire Theatre, whites entered and took all the designated white seats. The driver, James F. Blake, who had put Mrs. Parks off a bus twelve years earlier, now demanded that four black passengers, including Mrs. Parks, give up their seats to whites.

"Y'all better make it light on yourselves and let me have those seats," Blake demanded. Three blacks moved. Mrs. Parks stayed seated.

"Are you going to stand up?" Blake demanded.

"No."

"Well, I'm going to have you arrested."

"You may do that."

Why did Rosa Parks say "No"? Indeed she was physically tired at the end of the day, but she later said, "Our mistreatment was just not right, and I was tired of it. The more we gave in, the worse they treated us." She was being subjected to the same treatment that caused Frederick Douglass to resist going to Jim Crow cars on trains, that caused Gandhi serious difficulties when he attempted to travel first class in South Africa. Millions of people in the South, hundreds of millions worldwide, had been subjected to such humiliation, and a few had protested, even in the rigidly segregated South. But it was the incident in Montgomery that brought forth a protracted movement to end segregation and win civil rights for blacks in the United States.

Rosa McCauley, who was to spark this incident at the Empire Theatre, was born in 1913 in Tuskegee, Alabama, into a family that had a tradition of standing up for their rights. One of her grandfathers had light-colored skin and was often mistaken for white. He broke racial taboos and shook hands with whites and introduced himself using his family name. When the Klan was active near his house, her grandfather "would sit with his shotgun and say that he did not know how long he would last, but if they came breaking in . . . he was going to get the first one who came through the door. He never looked for trouble, but he believed in defending his home." His granddaughter wrote defiantly, "I saw and heard so much as a child growing up with hate and injustice against black people. I learned to put my trust in God and to seek Him as my strength. Long ago I set my mind to be a free person and not to give in to fear. I always felt that it was my right to defend myself if I could."

Rosa McCauley was forced to leave school because of illness in the family. In 1932 she married Raymond Parks, a barber, who was active in NAACP affairs and in defending the Scottsboro Boys, nine African Americans charged in 1931 with raping two white women prostitutes in a freight car. Convicted, some were sentenced to death and others to long prison terms. The U.S. Supreme Court twice reversed the convictions, and all nine defendants were eventually set free.

Raymond Parks encouraged Rosa to finish high school, and she did so in 1933, no small achievement for a black at a time when few blacks graduated from high school. But her diploma did not help her find more suitable employment, and she worked as a seamstress and as an office clerk. In 1943 she became the unpaid secretary of E. D. Nixon (1899–1987), a sleeping car porter, a union man, a supporter of A. Philip Randolph, and a leader in the Montgomery, Alabama, NAACP. Through her work with him, she was kept apprised of the problems of blacks throughout the South. She was determined to register to vote but faced years of disappointment and denial of her rights by recalcitrant registrars and discriminatary restrictions.

Rosa Parks also worked as a seamstress in the home of native Alabamians Clifford and Virginia Durr. The Durrs were white and well connected in official Washington circles in the 1930s and '40s, he serving on the Federal Communications Commission (FCC). They were unusual in those years in their firm support of the rights of blacks. Virginia Durr worked with Eleanor Roosevelt and chaired the Virginia committee for Henry Wallace's presidential campaign in 1948. She ran unsuccessfully for the Senate that year on the Progressive party ticket.

Clifford Durr was denied reappointment to the FCC in 1948 because he objected to the "loyalty oath," an instrument of anti-communism that especially affected government and the schools. Since he defended many radicals in his law practice, he was investigated by J. Edgar Hoover's FBI as a Communist. The Durrs returned to Montgomery in 1950, where Clifford Durr opened a law office. The Durrs were shunned by most of the white community; Durr's clients were largely black people who could not afford the usual legal fees. Rosa Parks became a family friend.

Virginia Durr recommended Parks for a summer scholarship in 1955 to the Highlander Folk School in Monteagle, Tennessee. Parks was to attend a two-week workshop on "Radical Desegregation: Implementing the Supreme Court Decision." Highlander was an integrated community that trained activists to work for "Racial Democracy" and "An Economically Just Society." The school was considered dangerous to the white powers of segregated Southern society, and it was harassed by the Klan and investigated by the FBI. Rosa Parks had been active in NAACP affairs, had occasionally served as an officer in the local organization, and was receptive to this advanced training. She successfully completed the Highlander workshop. She was the best possible person to defy the bus segregation statutes in Montgomery, for she was neatly dressed, well spoken, religious, and highly regarded in the black community.

When Rosa Parks refused to vacate her seat that day, the police were called to the bus still sitting in front of the Empire Theatre. (It is ironic that Gandhi's civil disobedience campaign in South Africa also began at an Empire Theatre.) Mrs. Parks was arrested, taken from the bus to jail, and booked. During that process she asked for a drink of water, but the water fountain was for whites only and her request was denied. She asked to use the telephone, but that was denied. She was placed in a cell with other women and finally allowed to call home and speak to her mother and husband. Their first concern was that she had been harmed, but she assured them that she had not. Her husband borrowed a car and left for the jail. E. D. Nixon was notified, and when he telephoned the police station to learn what charges had been lodged against her, the police refused to talk to him because he was black. He then asked Clifford Durr to call and find out what the charges were.

Durr was incensed that his friend had been arrested. He telephoned the jail immediately and learned she had violated the city's segregation laws. Bond was one hundred dollars. Durr, who had no paying clients, did not have the necessary funds, but Nixon, with his good position as a sleeping car porter, was able to pay the bond. He asked the Durrs to come to the jail with him, for he feared the police would take his money, deny having it, and leave Parks in jail. On the way to the jail, the three talked about using Rosa Parks in a test case against the segregated bus system. Other black women had been arrested on buses, but they were not good witnesses. Parks was a "Southern lady" in every respect—except for her color.

Rosa Parks was freed just as her husband arrived at the jail. Later, in the Parkses' living room, she was asked if she would be willing to be a part of a test case in the courts. She asked for time to think through the problem and the consequences of such action. If she agreed, she might be in physical danger. She might be fired from her job (she was), and they needed her income since her husband was not well paid as a barber. She conferred that night with her mother and her husband, who was afraid that white people would kill her.

Rosa Parks was a determined woman, opposed to segregation in all its aspects. She agreed to be part of the test case. How would the case be financed? The local NAACP had limited funds, and the Parks, Durr, and Nixon families could not afford to subsidize a long court battle. It was decided to approach the NAACP's Legal Defense and Educational Fund. A young black attorney in Montgomery, Fred Gray, was asked to take over the case. Clifford Durr would work behind the scenes because Supreme Court Justice Hugo Black was his brother-in-law, and Durr did not want Justice Black to have to recuse himself because of a conflict of interest should the case go all the way to the highest court.

Later that night Nixon gave an account of the arrest to Fred Gray, who had been out of town earlier in the day. Gray conferred with Rosa Parks before telephoning Professor Jo Ann Robinson of the English Department at Alabama State College, an historically black college in Montgomery. Robinson, a black woman, had been active in the Women's Political Council that had previously objected to the treatment of blacks on the city bus system, protests that had been ignored. She wanted to begin a boycott of the hated bus system, and with Nixon's approval she agreed to prepare leaflets to be distributed throughout the black community, calling for a boycott the following Monday, the day Rosa Parks was to be tried. She and friends worked through the night preparing the one-page text:

"Another Negro woman has been arrested and thrown into jail because she refused to get up out of her seat on the bus for a white person to sit down.

". . . Negroes have rights, too, for if Negroes did not ride the buses, they could not operate. . . . If we do not do something to stop these arrests, they will continue. The next time it may be you, or your daughter, or mother.

"The woman's case will come up on Monday. We are, therefore, asking every Negro to stay off the buses Monday in protest of the arrest and trial. Don't ride the buses to work, to town, to school, or anywhere on Monday.

". . . If you work, take a cab, or walk. But please, children and grown-ups, don't ride the bus at all on Monday. Please stay off all buses Monday."

The leaflets were mimeographed during the night and were ready for distribution early Friday morning.

At five o'clock Friday morning, Nixon, who had to leave that day for his job as a sleeping car porter, began making more telephone calls. His first was to Ralph Abernathy (1926–1990), the young minister of a large black Baptist church in the city. Abernathy was secretary of the Baptist Ministers' Alliance, and Nixon realized it was crucial to get the black ministers of Montgomery to support the boycott. A staunch opponent of segregation, Abernathy agreed to help and suggested that Nixon call his friend, the pastor of the Dexter Avenue Baptist Church, the Reverend Martin Luther King, Jr., to ask if a meeting of the Baptist Ministers' Alliance could be held at his church that night. The Dexter Avenue Baptist Church was centrally located.

"Brother Nixon," King responded, "let me think about it awhile, and call me back." King had a baby daughter only a few weeks old and many responsibilities in his church. He had completed his doctoral dissertation—"A Comparison of the Conceptions of God in the thinking of Paul Tillich and Henry Nelson Wieman"—and received his Ph.D. from Boston University in June 1955. He had his professional and family life to consider.

Nixon, a working-class man who moved more speedily than the scholarly King, felt a sense of urgency and called Ralph Abernathy to report the conversation. Abernathy then called King who said that he was not reluctant about the meeting, but he could not be the one to organize it because of his heavy schedule. The meeting, though, could certainly be held at his church.

Abernathy went back to making telephone calls. L. Roy Bennett, president of the black Interdenominational Alliance and minister of the Mt. Zion AME Church, agreed to preside at the meeting that evening in a basement room of King's church. Black community leaders gathered, but the session turned out to be a fiasco. Reverend Bennett apparently believed that he knew all about the organization of a boycott and talked nonstop. People began to leave. Finally, when only about twenty people were left, Abernathy took the floor from Bennett and proposed that others in the audience be allowed to speak. Professor Jo Ann Robinson seconded the motion and then proposed that those present endorse the Monday boycott. A mass meeting was then scheduled for Monday night to consider the success of the boycott and the possibility of extending it. King and Abernathy stayed at the church writing a new, shorter leaflet about the coming boycott and the Monday night mass meeting; it was mimeographed and ready for distribution the next day. The two then arranged for a brief meeting Monday afternoon to plan the Monday night gathering. Arrangements were made for black-owned taxi firms to carry boycotters that Monday for ten cents, the usual bus fare.

White citizens were learning about the boycott from their maids and from newspaper articles. Before Nixon left on his train run, he briefed the reporter Joe Azbell for a story in the *Montgomery Sunday Advertiser*. Nixon, with his NAACP experience, understood the value of getting the story out to the white community as well as to blacks.

On Monday morning blacks did not ride the buses. Some walked, some took taxis, others drove. The buses were virtually empty. The police overreacted and sent units to keep imaginary "goon squads" of blacks from intimidating would-be riders. The one-day protest was a success.

That same morning Rosa Parks was found guilty and fined ten dollars plus four dollars in court costs. Hundreds of blacks were at the courthouse to show their support. Fred Gray gave notice of appeal.

In December 1955, in Montgomery, Alabama, Rosa Parks refused to move to the back of the bus. *(Library of Congress)*

That afternoon several leaders in the black community met to plan for the mass meeting called for that night. Again it was a contentious meeting. Several realized that Reverend Bennett was unsuited to head their new protest group, which they named the Montgomery Improvement Association. Who would be president?

Ralph Abernathy would have been a strong choice. He was an effective speaker, but not polished. His church was not elite, and Montgomery's working-class blacks would have felt at ease with him. He had recently turned down the local NAACP presidency, for he was thinking of enrolling in graduate school.

He did complete a master's degree at Atlanta University in 1958. He worked closely with King in the years of struggle that followed.

E. D. Nixon was a proven leader in local and state NAACP affairs and would have enjoyed the backing of A. Philip Randolph and the Brotherhood of Sleeping Car Porters. He wanted the presidency of the new organization, but he was not an educated man and often spoke his mind with such force that he made enemies instead of bringing disparate black groups together.

Professor Jo Ann Robinson was articulate, energetic, and a proven organizer of earlier protests against segregation policies on Montgomery buses. Her position at Alabama State College would have been jeopardized if she had taken the leadership of the new organization. Certainly the budget of the college might be reduced by angry legislators. Perhaps more important, she would have to overcome the mind-set of black ministers who took major roles in such organizations as the Montgomery Improvement Association and tended to be male chauvinists who relegated women to nonleadership roles such as secretaries, assistants, choir directors, and leaders of groups for women and children.

Rosa Parks, the first hero of the struggle and a person of strong character, was well organized and smart about racial affairs, but she was shy and was never seriously considered for a major leadership position in Montgomery. The preachers in the movement never found ways to use her talents.

Fred Gray, the black attorney and a native of Montgomery, was respected by leaders in the black community. He would have worked well with the NAACP teams, but he was young (born in 1930) and probably was never seriously considered for the presidency.

Rufus Lewis, with a funeral home business, was a former librarian and football coach at Alabama State and had been active in black affairs in Montgomery, where he often competed with E. D. Nixon for leadership in the black community. Lewis was a member of the Dexter Avenue Baptist Church and favored his minister, Dr. King, for the leadership role in the association.

Martin Luther King, Jr., was certainly not the obvious choice for the presidency. He was young (born in 1929) and pastor of an elite church. Would he have a common touch? Could he lead maids, cooks, gardeners, day laborers, people denied an education? Members of the black middle class? White supporters? He had less experience than Nixon, Robinson, or Abernathy, and he did not covet new responsibilities.

In *Parting the Waters*, Taylor Branch describes a dramatic scene that took place at the late-afternoon planning session that Monday. The meeting was held at Bennett's church, and he chaired it. The group discussed some negotiating demands to be put forward to the bus company, but there followed suggestions about keeping secret the demands and the names of the leaders. Nixon was scathing in his response: "How do you think you can run a boycott in secret? Let me tell you gentlemen one thing. You ministers have lived off these washwomen for the last hundred years and ain't never done nothing for them." He threatened to expose the ministers at the night meeting for allowing women to break the law and be jailed while they themselves tried to work in secret. "We've worn aprons all our lives. It's time to take the aprons off. . . . If we're going to be mens, now's the time to be mens."

King arrived at the meeting as Nixon was ending this peroration and said, "Brother Nixon, I'm not a coward. I don't want anyone to call me a coward." This response clearly showed King in a positive light, but there is no reason to believe his words were part of a plan to seek the presidency of the newly formed group.

Rufus Lewis wanted to block Nixon as president and immediately nominated King. There were no other nominations. King was elected. He was new to Montgomery and without enemies. Taylor Branch adds a sentence to his account of the scene that cannot easily be ignored in light of Nixon's indictment of many accommodationist ministers: "Cynics would say that the established preachers stepped back for King only because they saw more blame and danger ahead than glory."

King had only a few minutes to prepare his address to be given that night at the Holt Street Baptist Church in a working-class section of the city. His speech was masterfully crafted, praising the civil disobedience of Rosa Parks and recounting in detail the mistreatment blacks had received on the city buses. He used the biblical language and the cadences of black sermons as he appealed to the disinherited to continue the boycott. He called for love, faith, and justice in pursuing the struggle. He had a smooth, powerful speaking voice, and his audience frequently responded with "Yes," "That's right," "Yeah," and applause.

Ralph Abernathy then proposed the following resolutions:

—That every person in the city stop riding buses until an arrangement could be worked out between the citizens and the bus company.

—That everyone with a car use it to transport workers at no charge.

—That employers of employees living at a great distance arrange transportation for their employees.

—That black citizens stood ready to send a delegation to meet with the management of the Montgomery City Lines to discuss grievances and solutions.

—That no unlawful means—including intimidation—would be used during the boycott.

The audience approved and clearly wanted the boycott to continue.

The next day the Montgomery Improvement Association wired the owners of the bus line making three proposals:

—That bus drivers treat passengers with courtesy.

—That black riders be seated from the back forward and white riders from the front to the back, with no seats reserved for whites or blacks.

—That black drivers be hired for routes predominantly serving black passengers.

These were modest demands. Nixon would have demanded more. But city and bus line officials made no concessions. The thirteen-month struggle was beginning.

Just who was the new president of the Montgomery Improvement Association?

Michael Luther King, Jr., was born in Atlanta, Georgia, on January 15, 1929, into a family with two prominent black ministers. His father, Michael Luther King (1897–1984), was born to sharecroppers and escaped rural poverty by moving to Atlanta where he worked at manual labor and completed high school. He felt a call to preach and began to minister to small churches; he attended and graduated from Morehouse College. He began to pay court to Alberta Williams, the daughter of Adam Daniel Williams, pastor of the Ebenezer Baptist Church, one of the most prestigious black churches in the city. Reverend Williams, a graduate of Morehouse College, delivered "hellfire and brimstone" sermons, but he was interested in more than "saving souls." As a supporter of civil rights for blacks, he was an active member of the NAACP and helped pressure the city of Atlanta into building the first high school for black students.

King and Alberta Williams were married in 1926 and moved into the home of her parents. Reverend Williams died in 1931, and King became pastor of Ebenezer Baptist Church. His sermons could be sulfurous, but he was also concerned about racial matters. Like his father-in-law, he was a local leader in NAACP affairs. He favored a voter registration drive for blacks, and he fought to equalize the salaries of black and white school teachers.

After the death of Williams, King purchased a large house for his family, which included two sons and one daughter. The Kings lived a middle-class life in segregated Atlanta. King changed his first name to Martin, also changing his son's name, no doubt choosing "Martin" to embellish his honor of Martin Luther, leader of the Protestant Reformation.

Much of Martin Luther King, Jr.'s early life was concerned with church matters and family affairs. The young King eventually became embarrassed by the emotionalism of his father's sermons, but he felt great affection for the strong-willed, patriarchal figure who ruled the household. As much as he loved his father, he needed to remove himself from his father's control, without causing a break in their relationship.

Young King attended the Morehouse Laboratory school until it closed; then he went to the segregated Atlanta public schools. In Atlanta the bus system, movie theaters, public rest rooms, bus and train waiting rooms, and drinking fountains were segregated. Shoe stores might insist that black patrons go to a specified section. Reverend King, confronted with such insulting service, took his son out of the store without making a purchase.

The young King entered the all-black Booker T. Washington High School in 1942. Bright and personable, he was interested in girls and dancing, even though dancing was frowned upon, even forbidden, by many Baptist churches. He had a good speaking voice and was quick to organize and present his ideas. In his junior year, in April 1944, he won a local oratorical contest speaking on "The Negro and the Constitution." He later represented his school at the statewide competition held in Dublin, Georgia, a contest he also won. He was accompanied by his speech teacher, Sarah Grace Bradley. During their return to Atlanta, King and his teacher were ordered to give up their seats on the bus to white passengers. King at first refused. The driver cursed him, calling him a "son-of-a-bitch," but his teacher convinced him to follow the orders of the driver. They stood the rest of the way, and King remembered many years later that he was the angriest he had ever been.

King skipped his senior year of high school. Dr. Mays, president of Morehouse College, was faced with declining enrollment during World War II and initiated an early-entry program for qualified students. King entered Morehouse at the age of fifteen and continued to live at home during his college years. He majored in sociology, minored in English, and took several courses in religion. He led an active social life but was hardly a brilliant scholar. His college transcript shows that he was, overall, a C+ to B− student.

Several of his teachers at Morehouse were ordained ministers who believed in the Social Gospel, a twentieth-century liberal movement in Protestant churches which applied biblical teachings to social problems. Mays, also a minister, was a proponent of the Social Gospel and was influenced as well by the Gandhian movement. King heard Mays's talks at chapel and often went to the president's office for discussions. Mays was also a friend of the King family and visited at their home. Because his father was a prominent minister and a friend of the college president, young King enjoyed a special position on campus. He was perhaps less studious than he might have been in other circumstances.

King's favorite undergraduate teacher, Professor George Kelsey, a theologian, was a proponent of the Social Gospel. Richard Chivers, King's adviser and a sociologist, studied the economic bases of racism. In his senior year, King enrolled in the two-semester Introduction to Philosophy taught by Samuel Williams, also a minister, who supported Henry A. Wallace and the People's Progressive party in Georgia in 1948. It was in that survey of the history of philosophy that King read Thoreau's essay "Civil Disobedience" for the first time. Later, in *Stride Toward Freedom*, King wrote, "Fascinated by the idea of refusing to cooperate with an evil system, I was so deeply moved that I reread the work several times. That was my first intellectual contact with the theory of nonviolent resistance."

In Professor Williams's course the participants studied Socrates, Moses, Machiavelli, Descartes, Kant, Hegel, Marx, and other great thinkers. King's interest in philosophy grew over the academic year. He received a C in the first semester and a B in the second. As Professor Williams remembered, King "came to Morehouse rather young, and it is not always the case that a student comes to full flower so young."

King decided during the summer of 1947 to become a minister. At that time and place, additional study beyond a bachelor's degree from Morehouse would not have been necessary, but King preferred to enter a seminary for advanced study after his graduation in 1948. His father wanted him to come to the Ebenezer Church to assist him, but he concurred with his son's wishes and provided financial support. When King entered the liberal Crozer Theological Seminary in Chester, Pennsylvania, for the first time in his life he became a serious student.

At Crozer he was just a year older than most first-year college students, and the Crozer students were several years older than he. In his third semester he began studying with George Washington Davis, who held a doctorate from Yale and was greatly influenced by Walter Rauschenbusch, a major proponent of the Social Gospel. King had heard some of those ideas at Morehouse from Mays and Kelsey. He made a special study of Rauschenbusch, and though King thought him too optimistic about the essential goodness of man, with minor adjustments he placed himself in the category of a minister of the Social Gospel.

King also turned to philosophical studies on his own. It appears he reread Plato (and therefore about Socrates), Rousseau, Hobbes, Bentham, Mill, and Locke. He could hardly have missed in these writers their philosophic concerns about human freedom and the power of dissent in the face of laws that seemed wrong.

During the 1949 Christmas holidays King studied Marx, but he rejected the materialist implications and totalitarianism of Marxism. As a committed Christian, he was strongly opposed to most Marxist tenets, but he did find value in Marx's concern for social justice and in his discussion of the disparities between those with wealth and those in deep poverty. Although certainly not a Marxist, King was acutely aware of the weaknesses of capitalism.

During his three years at Crozer, King studied the Bible from Genesis to Revelation. He read stories of slavery and freedom, love and hate, good and evil, blind submission to God's will or the will of the state, revolt from God and revolt from secular laws. Moses and David, Jesus and Paul, Noah and Job—King studied a remarkable cast of characters, events, and theological interpretations of this biblical literature. All of this he had to put somehow into twentieth-century perspective and compare it with the philosophies of thinkers as different as Socrates, Thoreau, and Gandhi.

Gandhism was discussed at Crozer in November of King's second year there. A. J. Muste (1885–1967), of the Fellowship of Reconciliation, a pacifist organization, and a follower of Gandhian nonviolence, spoke on pacifism. King and most of his fellow students were not convinced by Muste's presentation, believing war might be necessary to combat submission to a totalitarian state. It is not certain how extensive were the references to Gandhi's movement in Muste's speech, but civil disobedience was certainly mentioned.

King clearly had some interest in Gandhi. He drove to Philadelphia in the spring of 1950 to hear Mordecai Johnson, president of Howard University, speak on Gandhi at Fellowship House. Johnson, influenced by Rauschenbusch's Social Gospel and by Gandhi, had just returned from a forty-day trip to India.

"Why was Gandhi a great man?" Johnson asked in his speech. "He had liberated India. He did it without firing a shot. He embraced the Untouchables as children of God and made a place for them in a society that had excluded them, segregated them. For his exemplary and saintly personal life alone, he was a great man. But the capstone of it all . . . was this: he had shown how to harness the redemptive power of love to social issues, and through it, change had to come. He had even, like Jesus, died a redemptive death. . . ."

In his *Stride Toward Freedom*, King called the lecture "profound and electrifying," and he proceeded to buy half a dozen books by and about Gandhi. He does not name the titles, but two possibilities are Gandhi's *Autobiography*, then in a readily available edition published in 1948, and Louis Fischer's *The Life of Mahatma Gandhi*, published in 1950. Fellowship House would have had on sale various Quaker books and pamphlets about Gandhi.

King was especially moved by the account of Gandhi's Salt March to the sea in 1930. He probably read Fisher's dramatic chapter titled "Drama at the Seashore," which would surely have suggested to King that the nonviolent method could be used by blacks in the segregated South: "Gandhi did two things in 1930: he made the British people aware that they were cruelly subjugating India, and he gave Indians the conviction that they could, by lifting their hands and straightening their spines, lift the yoke from their shoulders. . . . The British beat the Indians with batons and rifle butts. The Indians neither cringed nor complained nor retreated. That made England powerless and India invincible."

King admitted that he had earlier thought that "love your enemies" was a valid philosophy applying only to individual conflict, but his reading of Gandhi convinced him that the nonviolent approach could be used on a massive scale. "Love for Gandhi," King wrote, "was a potent instrument for social and collective transformation. . . . I came to feel that this was the only morally and practically sound method open to oppressed people in their struggle for freedom." King's ideas about nonviolence and civil disobedience developed over a long period of time, and this statement in *Stride Toward Freedom* is his mature view. At Crozer, Gandhism was just one of many philosophies of interest to him.

After completing his three-year course at Crozer in 1951, King felt the need for still more study. His father would have preferred that his son return to Atlanta and assist him at Ebenezer, but he did agree to his son's entering the Boston University Ph.D. program in the fall of 1951. King was again a serious student of philosophy and religion, and he matured during his seminary and doctoral study. In his research papers he sometimes used sources improperly, but this went unnoticed by his professors. During his years in Boston he was even more drawn to the Social Gospel. He also met and married Coretta Scott from Alabama, who was studying music in Boston.

After King finished his course work, passed his doctoral exams, and selected a dissertation topic, he began searching for a pastorate. He did not wish to return to the love and control of his father in Atlanta; instead in 1954 he accepted the pastorate of the Dexter Avenue Baptist Church in Montgomery, Alabama. There he worked on his dissertation three hours each morning and then several hours at night. During the day he was fully involved in church affairs, tending the budget, making sick calls, preparing sermons and lectures. He also began to put into place many of his ideas derived from the Social Gospel. He established a Social and Political Action Committee with Jo Ann Robinson as co-chair. He set a goal of getting every adult member of the congregation registered to vote and enrolled as a member of the NAACP. He completed and submitted his dissertation in 1955, and his degree was awarded that June. The Kings' daughter, Yolanda Denise, was born in November that year.

When the bus boycott erupted in December 1955, King was thrust into a leadership role at a time when he was stressed and overworked at his church, while at home the baby cried and the telephone rang incessantly. He was, though, a determined and dedicated person, a forceful minister with a strong presence in the pulpit. He had a fine speaking voice, and he could present an anti-segregation argument to any audience.

In his stirring speech at the mass meeting on the night after the first day of the bus boycott, December 5, King did not

Martin Luther King, Jr., eating dinner with his family during the early days of the civil rights movement. Note the picture of Gandhi on the wall above. *(copyright Flip Schulke)*

mention Socrates, Thoreau, or Gandhi; instead he found justification for dissent against an unjust authority in the Christian
religion. Rather than invoke the theoretical knowledge of civil
disobedience he had learned at Morehouse, Crozer, and
Boston University, he relied on the power of love as found in
Christianity. His audience was overwhelmingly religious, and
undoubtedly his approach was the right one for the moment.

As the bus boycott continued, King and his close associates
put in long hours organizing participants and solving problems of transportation and car pools while dealing with vin-
dictive acts by the police. Added justification for the boycott
came on December 12, when the *Montgomery Advertiser*
printed a letter from Juliette Morgan, a white librarian: "The
Negroes of Montgomery," she wrote, "seem to have taken a
lesson from Gandhi—and our own Thoreau, who influenced
Gandhi. Their own task is greater than Gandhi's, however, for
they have greater prejudice to overcome. One feels that history
is being made in Montgomery these days. . . . It is hard to
imagine a soul so dead, a heart so hard, a vision so blinded
and provincial as not to be moved with admiration at the quiet
dignity, discipline and dedication with which the Negroes have
conducted their boycott." The letter reminded King of what he
had learned from his earlier academic study. Over a period of
time he was able to incorporate in new ways the ideas of
Thoreau and Gandhi into the Social Gospel and his own reading of the Sermon on the Mount.

At first Juliette Morgan's attitude found some white supporters, but leading white citizens and government officials
soon objected to her letter and her stand against segregation.
She was fired from her library position and lost most of her
friends. She did not survive the condemnation and in 1957 apparently took her own life.

Police stepped up their harassment of car-pool drivers, ticketing them for imaginary infractions. Jo Ann Robinson received thirty unjust tickets and paid them all. The police became part of the cabal to break the boycott. Black taxi drivers were told they had to charge boycotters the minimum fee of forty-five cents. On January 26, 1956, King himself was arrested for speeding. He was taken to jail and booked. He thought it likely he would be murdered by the police. Reverend Abernathy tried to bail him out but was unable to do so. When a large black crowd converged on the jail, the jailers panicked, and King was released on his own recognizance.

King received a steady stream of obscene telephone calls and threatening letters, but these were only a prelude to the bombing of his home on January 30, 1956. He was at a meeting when the bomb went off on the porch at the parsonage; his wife and daughter were not injured. When he arrived home, the police, some city officials, and a large crowd of blacks had gathered; there was the strong possibility of a riot. King urged his supporters to put their weapons aside, reminding them that Jesus had said, "Love your enemies." He was aware that he might be killed at any time, but he told his listeners that the movement must continue even if he were stopped. The crowd dispersed without violence. Stephen Oates, in his biography of King, quotes a policeman who was at the bombed house that night: "I'll be honest with you. I was terrified. I owe my life to that nigger Preacher, and so do all the other white people who were there."

Stories about the Montgomery boycott and its accompanying violence now began to appear in the national press. The Fellowship of Reconciliation, headed by A. J. Muste, whose speech on pacifism had not convinced King, decided to send Glenn Smiley, a white, Texas-born follower of Gandhi, to

Montgomery to teach nonviolent techniques. The black Quaker Bayard Rustin, long concerned with racial equality, also wanted to go to Montgomery to teach Gandhian techniques. Rustin was a skilled teacher, but he was an outsider and an agitator, and his past—his Communist youth, his homosexuality— meant that he had to be employed with caution.

Rustin arrived in Montgomery on Tuesday, February 21, 1956, the same day that more than a hundred participants in the local movement were indicted in state court for engaging in a boycott, forbidden by Alabama law. King was out of town, but Rustin met with Abernathy and E. D. Nixon. He learned that Abernathy's home too had been bombed, and that black guards, some of whom were armed, were in place around the homes of King and Abernathy.

Rustin met King for the first time on Thursday, February 23, and the two men began to discuss Gandhian tactics. Rustin later told an interviewer that King was not a developed Gandhian when the bus boycott began: "The glorious thing is that he came to a profoundly deep understanding of nonviolence through the struggle itself, and through readings and discussions which he had in the process of carrying on the protest, not that, in some way, college professors who had read Gandhi had prepared him in advance. This is just a hoax." Rustin did play an important role in teaching Gandhian, nonviolent techniques to the protesters in Montgomery, but he underestimates King's earlier philosophical readings of Gandhi and Thoreau. It is likely that King was a good listener and let Rustin explain Gandhian thought and practice without revealing his own knowledge. Rustin needed to declare his own importance and influence in the civil rights movement beginning in Montgomery. And another Gandhian was talking to King: Smiley gave King a copy of Gregg's *The Power of Nonviolence* at this time, and Smiley proved to be an effective teacher of the strategy.

Rustin told King that most of Gandhi's followers were not firm believers in Gandhian principles but that they nevertheless thought nonviolent civil disobedience was effective. This was obviously true among many of King's followers too. Rosa Parks wrote admiringly of her grandfather's willingness to use a gun to protect his home. She was an admirer of King, but she also believed in self-defense. Rustin clearly helped King and the organizers around him, but when the press began trying to learn more about Rustin, he became a danger to the Montgomery Improvement Association and was recalled to New York. King continued to regard Rustin as a valued consultant, and over the years they met and corresponded.

In discussing civil disobedience after it had been more fully developed, King argued that the term "passive resistance" was inaccurate, for the resisters were active, not passive, and they were certainly not cowards. (Gandhi had made some of these same objections to the term.) King also insisted that opponents were to be won over, not hated or harassed, and that the methods used by the nonresistants were designed to awaken the moral and ethical concerns of their opponents. In the end, he envisioned reconciliation and a community at peace.

King believed those in the movement should accept punishment without resisting and go to jail for breaking unjust laws. He also argued that the resister must avoid psychological violence by not hating his opponents. A believer in loving one's enemy, King argued that this love was not weak or sentimental; "Love in this connection means understanding, redemptive goodwill."

The willingness of Montgomery's blacks to abandon violence was severely tested by the bombings of homes of ministers and supporters of the movement, and of churches. It was difficult to stand firm and peaceful against the constant harassment of blacks and the complicity of the police in criminal acts against them. But they did.

Jo Ann Robinson had been receiving threatening calls, and Fred Gray and his wife were visiting her when a brick was thrown through her picture window. The man next door saw what happened, took the license number of the car, but did not know, Robinson says, that the police were behind the incident.

The neighbor drove to the police station and reported the violence to the police commissioner. He said, "I was looking at them when they threw this brick in that woman's window."

"Listen here, boy, do you want to live?"

"Yes, sir."

"Then go back home and shut your mouth."

Two weeks later Robinson heard noises at her carport and saw two policemen pouring something on her new car. The next morning she found acid holes on the top and the hood. At first she was infuriated, but then she decided, "these are beautiful spots." Asked about her damaged car, she would say, "Well, the police threw the acid on it, and burned it up, but it became beauty spots." Many others suffered much more than she did.

The Montgomery boycott went on for months. Workshops on nonviolence helped keep the members of the Montgomery Improvement Association from resorting to violence. King and other pastors praised nonviolence in their sermons and speeches. King was able to speak directly to his audiences. He did not talk down to his listeners, but he used language and biblical imagery they understood. The police acted ruthlessly as they and the city fathers and bus officials tried to break the will of the blacks. The Montgomery Improvement Association suffered one crisis after another, and the local judicial system routinely ruled against black protesters, but King kept urging the boycotters not to give up. He learned to be stoical in jail, as Thoreau and Gandhi had been.

On November 13, 1956, the Supreme Court ruled that state and local laws requiring segregation on buses were unconstitutional. The battle won in the courts, the nonviolent movement was now ready to move to a national stage. Its major features were in place. Ideas from Moses, Thoreau, and Gandhi were mingled with ideas from the Sermon on the Mount. The struggle would be longer and more difficult than the bus boycott had been, but nonviolent civil disobedience helped bring about fundamental change in the United States during the years following the boycott until 1968, when Martin Luther King, Jr., was assassinated.

We have not attempted to retell in great detail the Montgomery bus boycott and King's later career as a civil rights activist. Our goal has been to show how the concept of civil disobedience developed in a specific environment. The movement in the following years—the marches, the jailings, the murders, the successes, the failure of Dr. King in Chicago, the dissent over the Vietnam War—have been covered well by biographers such as Stephen Oates, Peter Ling, and others; by Taylor Branch in *Parting the Waters: America in the King Years, 1954–63* and *Pillar of Fire: America in the King Years, 1963–65*; by David J. Garrow's *Bearing the Cross: Martin Luther King, Jr., and the Southern Christian Leadership Conference* and *The FBI and Martin Luther King, Jr.*; plus other specialized studies over the years since King's death.

Dr. King leads a march in Alabama in 1965. *(Library of Congress)*

Out of his struggle for civil rights, out of the centuries-long struggle for freedom beginning with the introduction of slaves into Jamestown, Dr. King had a dream: "I have a dream that one day this nation will rise up and live out the true meaning of its creed: 'We hold these truths to be self-evident; that all men are created equal.'"

"Go blow dem ram horns."

Let the walls of prejudice come tumbling down.

Let the dream come true.

CHAPTER

IX

A BETTER DAY

There's a better day a coming—
There's a better day a coming—
Oh, Glory, Hallelujah!
—From "There's a Better Day a Coming"

❧ Jasper is a Southern town in the piney woods of east Texas. About half its 8,200 citizens are white, about half black. On a Saturday night in June 1998, a black man named James Byrd, Jr., was chained to the back of a pickup truck by three young white men and brutally dragged to his death. It might have been expected that the murder would be covered up and that protests—marches violent or nonviolent by black citizens—would be ignored. But that did not happen. The three perpetrators were prosecuted. Much had changed since the civil disobedience campaign in the South began outside the Empire Theatre in 1955.

The Montgomery bus boycott; the formation of the Southern Christian Leadership Conference pressing for civil rights; the lunch-counter demonstrations that began in Greensboro, North Carolina, in 1960 and spread to other cities; the Freedom

Rides of 1961; the use of dogs against children civil disobedients in Birmingham, Alabama; the 1963 March on Washington
where King gave his "I Have a Dream" speech—these and other
events influenced public opinion and led to the Civil Rights Act
of 1964, which called for the desegregation of public accommodations and banned discrimination in hiring and firing. Because blacks continued to have difficulties in registering to vote,
one year later Congress passed the Civil Rights Act of 1965, restricting educational requirements for voting and allowing federal registrars to enroll voters.

King's own voice was stilled in 1968 with his murder, and
massive civil disobedience by blacks ceased, but King's message, his technique of using mass demonstrations peacefully,
became part of the King story presented at the King Center
for Nonviolent Social Change in Atlanta and the King His-
toric District (the house where he was born, the crypt where
he is buried, the Ebenezer Baptist Church). The story of Martin Luther King, Jr., is retold during Black History Month
each February. King, his movement, his Nobel Prize for Peace,
his assassination have become a part of American history—
institutionalized, made acceptable to a large audience. The
King revolution remains in its near-original form in many
black churches.

Jasper is still a Southern town, but it has been changed by
King's movement and by the Civil Rights Acts of 1964 and
1965. Blacks now vote in the county, and the white sheriff at
the time of the murder of James Byrd was Billy Rowles, known
for being fair to blacks and whites. He also had strong ties to
black ministers in the community. Sheriff Rowles was badly
shaken when he saw Byrd's mangled body. "I had dreams
about him screaming," he said. "I could hear the sound of his
body dragging against the pavement."

When he left the crime scene on Huff Creek Road, Sheriff
Rowles called on Byrd's parents, prayed with them, and told
them, "We won't rest until we catch the men who did this to
your son."

The sheriff kept his word to the Byrd family, and he upheld
his oath of office. By early Monday morning he had arrested
three white suspects, two of whom were ex-convicts and white
supremacists.

It was a time of great stress in Jasper, for the brutal murder was news around the world. Several circumstances helped
prevent the eruption of violence. The mayor of Jasper was
black, and he established a committee to discuss race relations.
Meetings were held in the local churches to discuss racial attitudes and problems. The Ministerial Alliance was integrated
and urged restraint. The Byrd family acted with great dignity.

The minister of the Huff Creek Community Church has
said, "If a different sheriff had been in charge, we would've
had an unsolved hit-and-run, and that would've been the end
of it." The citizens of Jasper could see that the sheriff acted de-
cisively, and the district attorney vigorously prosecuted the
three men and won convictions. Two men were sent to death
row (death sentences are not part of the nonviolence creed, but
Jasper is in Texas, and Texas has a strong pro-execution bias),
and the third was given a life sentence.

Clearly some things had changed for the better in Jasper.
White killers of a black man were captured, prosecuted, and
convicted. But the Reverend Ray Charles Lewis complains that
the task force "spent a lot of time identifying problems, but
they didn't take any action. The town meetings made white
people more sensitive to what we face, but what came out of
them? What really changed?" Reverend Lewis concluded,
"What black people need is a fair shot at jobs and loans."

At the opening high school football game in Jasper in the
fall of 2003, whites filled the reserve section at the stadium
and blacks the general admission section. Pamela Colloff, who
wrote about Jasper, observed: "So dramatic was the division
that it appeared, at first glance, to be by design, as if the past
half-century had folded back on itself and the days of man-
dated segregation had returned."

Dr. King's dream "that all men are created equal" is still a
dream. In spite of *Brown v. Board of Education*, many schools
are still segregated. Racial profiling persists. Police brutality
has not ended. Too many blacks are out of work, too many are
in prison. Civil disobedience to oppose injustice is largely dor-
mant, though at times there are small-scale and individual
protests. Once again, much of the activity to ensure equal
rights for black people is to be found in the courts.

At the end of "Civil Disobedience," Thoreau asked two
pertinent questions: "Is a democracy, such as we know it, the
last improvement possible in government? Is it not possible to
take a step further towards recognizing and organizing the
rights of man?" He answered with his own dream: A state
which could afford to be just to everyone.

Why not?

Socrates said to the Athenians: ". . . The state is a great and
noble steed who is tardy in his motions owing to his very size,
and requires to be stirred into life. I am that gadfly which God
has attached to the state, and all day long and in all places am
always fastening upon you, arousing and persuading and re-
proaching you."

A better day was not coming to the Athenians, for they
chose to kill their gadfly.

George Washington's slave named Tom had a dream and
ran away. Captured. No better day for him in Barbados.

"Sukey" had a dream and ran away. A better day came for her, but her sons were returned to slavery.

Shadrach ran away from his fiery furnace. A better day came in Canada.

Corporal Cravat had a dream of equal pay and went to jail. A better payday was coming.

Rosa Parks believed in equality and was jailed. A better day was coming.

Mahatma Gandhi had a dream: "I wish I could persuade everybody that civil disobedience is the inherent right of a citizen. We dare not give it up without ceasing to be a man." There's a better day a-coming.

Dr. King had a dream still only partially realized. Why not now?

A NOTE ON SOURCES

Introduction: Why Not Every Man?

The lines from "Didn't My Lord Deliver Daniel" are from Patricia Liggins Hill, general ed., *Call and Response* (Boston: Houghton Mifflin, 1998), p. 47. We added the question mark at the end of the last line.

For background information on civil disobedience in Socrates, Jesus, Locke, Thoreau, Gandhi, and King, we have used the immensely helpful Curtis Crawford, ed., *Civil Disobedience: A Casebook* (New York: Crowell, 1973). Crawford does not discuss Moses. His comments on Jesus as a disobedient are on pp. 35–37.

We have used the King James version of the Bible throughout this study. Chapter and verse references are in the text.

The quotation from Locke is from *Two Treatises of Civil Government*, reprinted in Crawford, *Civil Disobedience*, p. 117.

Information about the revisions of the Declaration of Independence, including some lines about slavery deleted from the document, are from John Hope Franklin and Alfred A. Moss, Jr., *From Slavery to Freedom: A History of African Americans*, 8th ed. (New York: Knopf, 2003), p. 83.

Accounts of the Thoreau family as abolitionists are from Walter Harding, *The Days of Henry Thoreau* (New York: Knopf, 1965), *passim*.

Dr. King on holding broken communities together is from his *Stride Toward Freedom* (New York: Harper, 1958), p. 106.

Chapter I. Slavery and Civil Disobedience from Colonial Times to 1830

The lines from "Many Thousand Gone" are from Hill, *Call and Response*, p. 238.

Background information on slaves in the early Colonial period is from Franklin and Moss, *From Slavery to Freedom*, especially Chapter 4, pp. 64–78. The quote about the proposed execution of slaves found forty miles north of Albany is on p. 73. The quote about slavery not being successful in the Middle Colonies is from p. 75. The quote about slavery in the New England colonies is from p. 76.

Information about the end of slaveowning among Quakers is from Ben Richmond, "Foreword" to *Reminiscences of Levi Coffin* (Richmond, Ind.: Friends United Press, 1991), pp. xvi–xvii.

The 1643 New England Confederation statement concerning escaped slaves is from Wilbur H. Siebert, *The Underground Railroad from Slavery to Freedom* (1898), reprinted (New York: Russell & Russell, 1967), p. 19.

The account of the escape of slaves from George Washington's estate is from Henry Wiencek, *An Imperfect God: George Washington, His Slaves, and the Creation of America* (New York : Farrar, Straus and Giroux, 2003), pp. 100–102. The account of Washington's sale of Tom is on pp. 131–132. The direct quotes about the sale are also from those two pages.

Darlene Clark Hine, William C. Hine, and Stanley Harrold, *The African-American Odyssey* (Upper Saddle River, N.J.: Prentice Hall, 2000) has information about maroons in Florida, p. 66, as do Franklin and Moss, *From Slavery to Freedom*, p. 72.

The quotation about Douglass's moral code is from his "The Heroic Slave," in George Hendrick and Willene Hendrick, eds., *Two Slave Rebellions at Sea* (St. James, N.Y.: Brandywine Press, 2000), p. 31.

The quotation from Woolman is from his *Journal*, reprinted in Nina Baym, ed., *The Norton Anthology of American Literature* (New York: W. W. Norton, 1998), I:603. Whitehead's quotation about Woolman is from I:597.

The quotation from James Forten on the Declaration of Independence and the Constitution is from Herbert Aptheker, ed., *A Documentary History of the Negro People in the United States* (Secaucus, N.Y.: Citadel Press, 1951), I:60.

The quotes from Gouverneur Morris are from Richard Brookhiser, *Gentleman Revolutionary: Gouverneur Morris, The Rake Who Wrote the Constitution* (New York: Free Press, 2003), p. 85.

Quotations about the three-fifths compromise are from Garry Wills, *"Negro President": Jefferson and the Slave Power* (Boston: Houghton Mifflin, 2003), pp. 2–5.

For the information on Toussaint L'Ouverture and DuBois's comments on him, see Franklin and Moss, *From Slavery to Freedom*, pp. 101–102. On Quakers and others trying to stop the slave trade, pp. 102–103.

The list of Northern states abolishing slavery is from Hine, Hine, and Harrold, *African-American Odyssey*, p. 94.

The account of John Fairfield is from Coffin's *Reminiscences*, reprinted in George and Willene Hendrick, eds., *Fleeing for Freedom* (Chicago: Ivan R. Dee, 2004), pp. 78–90. Fairfield's quote about stealing slaves is from p. 79.

Quotations from the letters of George Washington about escaped slaves are from Siebert, *Underground Railroad*, p. 33.

The two quotations about the origin of the term Underground Railroad are from Larry Gara, *The Liberty Line: The Legend of the Underground Railroad* (Lexington: University of Kentucky Press, 1967), pp. 174, 144n.

Information about Reverend John Rankin is from Ann Hagedorn, *Beyond the River: The Untold Story of the Heroes of the Underground Railroad* (New York: Simon and Schuster, 2002). The quotation about Rankin needing to leave the state if he wants to discuss slavery is from p. 29.

The Emerson quotation from *Nature* is reprinted in Baym, *Norton Anthology of American Literature*, I:1075.

Thoreau on being a yogi is from Arthur C. Christy, *The Orient in American Transcendentalism* (New York: Columbia University Press, 1932), p. 201.

For an excellent discussion of the *Bhagavad-Gita*, see Christy, *Orient in American Transcendentalism*, pp. 23–29.

Thoreau read the 1785 edition of the *Bhagvat-Geeta*, translated by Charles Wilkins (London: C. Nourse), reprinted with an introduction by George Hendrick (Gainesville, Fla.: Scholars' Facsimiles and Reprints, 1959).

Hine, Hine, and Harrold, in *African-American Odyssey*, provide information about David Walker and Henry Highland Garnet. For information on David Ruggles, see two articles by Graham Russell Hodges: in *American National Biography*, 19:53–54, and in http://www.freedomforum.org/publications/msj/courage.summer2000/yo2.html.

Chapter II. Abolitionists, 1830–1861

The text of "Follow the Drinking Gou'd" is from Hill, *Call and Response*, p. 238.

Information about the major groups of nonviolent abolitionists is from Carleton Mabee, *Black Freedom* (New York: Macmillan, 1970), pp. 1–6. The four principles of the Nonresistance Society are quoted on p. 70.

The account of Lear Green's escape is from William Still's *The Underground Rail Road*, sections of which are printed in Hendrick, *Fleeing for Freedom*, pp. 160–162. The quotation is from p. 162.

For information about Douglass we have used William S. McFeely, *Frederick Douglass* (New York: W. W. Norton, 1991).

For Still's account of Henry Box Brown, see Hendrick, *Fleeing for Freedom*, pp. 108–116. The *New York Tribune* article is on pp. 113–116.

For information about Brown and the two Smiths, see Richard Newman, ed., *Narrative of the Life of Henry Box Brown* (New York: Oxford University Press, 2002), pp. xi–xxxii. Brown's comment on Smith's failure to travel with the box to Philadelphia is on p. 61.

The quotes from Harriet Jacobs are from George and Willene Hendrick, eds., *Incidents in the Life of a Slave Girl* (St. James, N.Y.: Brandywine Press, 1999), pp. 119, 124. The scholarly edition of *Incidents* was edited by Jean Fagan Yellin (Cambridge, Mass.: Harvard University Press, 2000). Yellin has also written *Harriet Jacobs: A Life* (New York: Basic Civitas Books, 2004).

Information about Ruggles is from Graham Russell Hodges's article in *American National Biography*, 19:53–54. Hodges's longer piece on Ruggles is found at http://ww.freedomforum.org/publications/msj/courage.summer2000/y02.html, where the quote about Cornish's turning against Ruggles appears on p. 5.

For Ruggles's troubles with public transportation, see Mabee, *Black Freedom*, pp. 113–115. For the account of the end of segregation on the Eastern Railroad, see. p. 125. For the three instances of segregation in churches, see p. 128. The number of black churches in New York and Philadelphia is from p. 133.

For the account of Douglass and his problems with his daughter's schools, see McFeely, *Frederick Douglass*, pp. 160–161.

For Douglass's attempts to desegregate the Rochester, N.Y., public schools, see Mabee, *Black Freedom*, pp. 160–161. For an account of Robert Purvis' refusing to pay school taxes, see pp. 265–266. For reasons to boycott slave goods, see p. 189.

Chapter III. Civil Disobedience and Jim Crow Railroad Cars

The quote from Douglass at the beginning of the chapter is from his *My Bondage and My Freedom* (New York: Washington Square Press, 2003), p. 301.

For biographical information about Collins, we used Mabee, *Black Freedom*, pp. 76, 80–82, 119. Garrison's quotation about Collins is from p. 119. See also the biographical sketch on Collins in *American National Biography*, 5:253–254.

For the account of the meeting of Douglass and Collins, see Douglass, *My Bondage and My Freedom*, pp. 269–270. For Douglass on segregated churches, pp. 265–266.

The account of David Ruggles turning to the courts for redress after he was ordered to move from an all-white railroad car is from Mabee, *Black Freedom*, pp. 113–114.

The Douglass-Buffum relationship is discussed in McFeely, *Frederick Douglass*, pp. 120–123. Webb's letter is from p. 121.

Douglass's statement on not going into Jim Crow cars is from *My Bondage and My Freedom*, p. 302.

Stephen A. Chase's being called "Bulldog of Prejudice" is from Mabee, *Black Freedom*, p. 120. The account of William Bassett being expelled from the Friends is on pp. 73, 120. Buffum's account of the effects of the demonstrations is from p. 121. Mrs. Mary Greene's letter to railroad stockholders is from p. 117.

The quotation from Thoreau's "Civil Disobedience" is from Baym, *Norton Anthology of American Literature*, I:1754.

Douglass's account of the settlement of incidents arising from segregation on New England railroads is from his *My Bondage and My Freedom*, p. 303.

Chapter IV. Danger: "Have Top Eye Open"

The words from "KIDNAPPERS AND SLAVE CATCHERS" poster of 1851 are reproduced from Hine, Hine, and Harrold, *African-American Odyssey*, p. 211.

Carol Pirtle found the papers of the Hayes family and wrote about the "Sukey" case in detail in *Escape Betwixt Two Suns: A True Tale of the Underground Railroad in Illinois* (Carbondale: Southern Illinois University Press, 2000). Our information and quotes about this case are drawn from this book.

Biographical information about Cross is from Dwight Lowell Drummond, *Anti-Slavery: The Crusade for Freedom in America* (Ann Arbor: University of Michigan Press, 1961), p. 186.

For the details of the Shadrach story we are indebted to Gary Collison's excellent *Shadrach Minkins: From Fugitive Slave to Citizen* (Cambridge, Mass.: Harvard University Press, 1997).

Irving H. Bartlett, in *Daniel Webster* (New York: W. W. Norton, 1978), has a good discussion of the Compromise of 1850, pp.

240–253. Also useful are Franklin and Moss, *From Slavery to Freedom*, pp. 176–178; Hine, Hine, and Harrold, *African-American Odyssey*, pp. 186–187, 206–207; and Siebert, *Underground Railroad*, pp. 361–366. The text of the Fugitive Slave Act of 1850 is reproduced on those pages.

Hine, Hine, and Harrold, in *African-American Odyssey*, p. 206, have a good, brief discussion of the Wilmot Proviso.

Biblical references are to the King James version, widely used in the nineteenth-century United States.

On the attempt to capture William and Ellen Craft, we have also used R. J. M. Blackett, "The Odyssey of William and Ellen Craft," in his edition of their *Running a Thousand Miles for Freedom* (Baton Rouge: Louisiana State University Press, 1999), pp. 58–62.

Thoreau's enigmatic comments about Shadrach are quoted by Collison on pp. 157–158 from *The Writings of Henry D. Thoreau: Journal* (Princeton: Princeton University Press, 1990–), 3:194.

Biographical information about Sims and his capture are from Collison, *Shadrach Minkins*, p. 190; and Albert J. von Frank, *The Trials of Anthony Burns* (Cambridge, Mass.: Harvard University Press, 1998), pp. 27–29. The Higginson quotation is from von Frank, p. 28.

The quotations from Daniel Webster about Sims and from Webster's public statement in Boston are from Bartlett, *Daniel Webster*, p. 264.

Collison describes the trials of those who helped Sims in *Shadrach Minkins*, pp. 192–196.

Information about Sims's later life is from John W. Blassingame, ed., *Slave Testimony* (Baton Rouge: Louisiana State University Press, 1977), pp. 92–93.

Biographical information about Henry Williams is from Collison, *Shadrach Minkins*, p. 158.

Information about Williams with the Thoreaus is from Harding, *Days of Henry Thoreau*, pp. 315–317.

Information about Levi Coffin and his wife and William Still and his wife is from Hendrick, *Fleeing for Freedom*.

For information about the Kansas-Nebraska Act, we have used Hine, Hine, and Harrold, *African-American Odyssey*, pp. 214–215.

For background information and details on the rescue of Jerry Henry, we have used von Frank, *Trials of Anthony Burns*.

Background information about Daniel Webster is from Bartlett, *Daniel Webster*.

Information about the Liberty Party is from McFeely, *Frederick Douglass*, pp. 106–107.

The story of Louis is told in Levi Coffin, *Reminiscences* (Cincinnati: Western Tract Society, 1876), pp. 548–553.

Biographical information about the early life of Anthony Burns and other details of his story are from von Frank, *Trials of Anthony Burns*.

The size of the Boston Vigilance Committee is from Mabee, *Black Freedom*, p. 309. Whittier's quote about a march is on pp. 308–309.

The account of the vigil in front of the hotel where Suttle was staying is from Mabee, *Black Freedom*, p. 310.

For the story of Anthony Bryant and Dr. Hiram Rutherford, see George Hendrick and Willene Hendrick, *On the Illinois Frontier* (Carbondale: Southern Illinois University Press, 1981). The account of the Methodist minister who would not help Bryant is on p. 132.

Harding discusses the differences in "Civil Disobedience" and "Slavery in Massachusetts" in his *Days of Henry Thoreau*, pp. 318–319.

The quotation from "Slavery in Massachusetts" is from Baym, *Norton Anthology of American Literature*, I:1747.

Background information about Dred Scott is from Hine, Hine, and Harrold, *African-American Odyssey*, pp. 215–217. The quotation from Taney is on p. 216.

Chapter V. From the Civil War Through Reconstruction: The End of Slavery

The chorus of "Joshua Fit de Battle of Jericho" is from *Call and Response*, p. 47.

The quotation by General Butler, and information about the First Confiscation Act, is from Franklin and Moss, *From Slavery to Freedom*, p. 222.

The quote from General McClellan is from Hine, Hine, and Harrold, *African-American Odyssey*, pp. 230–231. Information about the contraband policy of General Grant and the Fremont-Lincoln controversy over freeing Missouri slaves is from p. 231.

The Mary Chestnut quotation is from William Loren Katz, *Breaking the Chains* (New York: Atheneum, 1990), p. 144. The Emily Douglass quote is from p. 152.

Levi Coffin on escapees being shot is from his *Reminiscences*, p. 630.

Charlotte Forten on Michael's attempt to escape is from her *Journal*, parts of which appeared in Richard Barksdale and Keneth Kinnamon, *Black Writers of America* (New York: Macmillan, 1972), p. 301.

The quote from General Saxton is from Katz, *Breaking the Chains*, pp. 148–149.

Yellin writes perceptively about contrabands in *Harriet Jacobs: A Life*. The quotes about Reverend Gladwin are from pp. 165 and 171.

Levi Coffin in his *Reminiscences* writes about the white refugee Southerners, pp. 642–643.

The biographical sketch and portions of letters by Cravat to his wife are from Barksdale and Kinnamon, *Black Writers of America*, pp. 263–266. The late Professor Barksdale was a descendant of Corporal Cravat.

Information about pay for privates in the Union army and the subsequent act to equalize pay is from Franklin and Moss, *From Slavery to Freedom*, p. 239.

Background information about Robert Smalls is from the entry on Smalls in *American National Biography*, 20:111–112, and Edward A. Miller, Jr., *Gullah Statesman: Robert Smalls from Slavery to Congress, 1839–1915* (Columbia: University of South Carolina Press, 1995), pp. 1–10. All the direct quotations are from *Gullah Statesman*. See also an interview with Smalls reprinted in Blassingame, *Slave Testimony*, pp. 373–379.

The Thoreau quotation is from "Civil Disobedience" in Baym, *Norton Anthology of American Literature*, I:1755.

The quotation from the *Columbia Guardian* is from Miller, *Gullah Statesman*, pp. 5–6.

Background information on the Reconstruction is from Franklin and Moss, *From Slavery to Freedom*, and Hine, Hine, and Harrold, *African-American Odyssey*. We have used the detailed chronology in Lerone Bennett, Jr., *Before the Mayflower: A History of Black America*, Millennium Edition (Chicago: Johnson Publishing, 2003), pp. 457–719.

Background information about the early days of the Ku Klux Klan is from Wyn Craig Wade, *The Fiery Cross: The Ku Klux Klan in America* (New York: Simon and Schuster, 1987), pp. 31–53. On the Klan's reign of terror, see pp. 54–79. The account of the Klan, Champion, and the Bowdens is given on pp. 69–71. On the sexual element in "Kluxing" and the rape of Mrs. Gilmore's daughter, see p. 76.

Chapter VI. Thoreau's Essay Travels Across the Oceans to Gandhi

Gandhi's comments on the plight of Indians in South Africa are from his *Speeches and Writings* (Madras: Natesan, 1918[?]), pp. 4–5. Biographical information about Gandhi's early life is from his *Autobiography: The Story of My Experiments with Truth* (Washington, D.C.: Public Affairs Press, 1948). For biographical information we have also consulted D. G. Tendulkar, *Mahatma*, 8 vols. (New Delhi: Publications Division, Government of India, 1951–1954); Pyarelal, *Mahatma Gandhi: The Early Phase* (Ahmedabad: Navajivan Publishing House, 1965); and *Mahatma Gandhi: The Last Phase*, 2 vols. (Ahmedabad: Navajivan Publishing House, 1956, 1958); Robert Payne, *The Life and Death of Mahatma Gandhi* (New York: E. P. Dutton, 1969); Judith M. Brown, *Gandhi: Prisoner of Hope* (New Haven: Yale University Press, 1989); and Louis Fischer, *The Life of Mahatma Gandhi* (New York: Harper, 1950).

Gandhi's misspelling of "kettle" is from his *Autobiography*, pp. 15–16.

Gandhi devotes several chapters in his *Autobiography* to his years in London. He discusses *The Song Celestial*, pp. 90–91. His comments on the Sermon on the Mount are on p. 92.

Gandhi gives a shortened version of his years in South Africa in his *Autobiography*. He has a more extensive account in *Satyagraha in South Africa* (Ahmedabad: Navajivan Publishing House, 1928). We have used both. We have also used the microfilm copies of the issues of *Indian Opinion* published during Gandhi's years in South Africa; this microfilm is in the library of the University of Texas at Austin. George Hendrick originally used these files in *Thoreau and Gandhi: A Study of the Development of "Civil Disobedience" and Satyagraha* (Ph.D. dissertation, University of Texas, 1954).

The account of Gandhi's troubles on the train is from his *Autobiography*, pp. 140–142. The account of the trip on the stage coach is from pp. 143–144. On the significance of the bill restricting the right of Indians to vote, p. 174. On Gandhi's supposedly unmerited condemnation of Natal citizens, p. 234.

Gandhi on the Zulu rebellion, his *Autobiography*, pp. 385–386.

The quotations from Generals Botha and Smuts are from Fischer, *Life of Mahatma Gandhi*, p. 57.

Gandhi writes about the Black Act in *Satyagraha in South Africa*, pp. 151–160. Gandhi's speech at the Empire Theatre is from pp. 164–169. His statement on Hindus and Muslims believing in the same God is from p. 165. His comments on sanctions that civil disobedients might face are on pp. 167–168. Gandhi on the deputation in 1906 to London is from pp. 182–193. He describes the scene at the permit office on pp. 210–214.

Gandhi's letter to the Rand *Daily Mail* is reproduced in *Indian Opinion*, July 6, 1907, p. 254. Gandhi's appeal to a "higher law" is from *Indian Opinion*, September 28, 1907, p. 340.

Gandhi's letter to his son suggesting that he read Emerson is reproduced in Fischer, *Life of Mahatma Gandhi*, p. 93.

Gandhi's mention of Thoreau in an article about the Archbishop of Canterbury and civil disobedience is from *Indian Opinion*, September 7, 1907, p. 364. That article is printed in *The*

Collected Works of Mahatma Gandhi (Delhi: Publications Division, Government of India, 1962), VII:211–212.

Gandhi's letter to Henry Salt about Thoreau, October 12, 1929, is reprinted in George and Willene Hendrick, eds., *The Savour of Salt: A Henry Salt Anthology* (Fontwell, Sussex, UK: Centaur Press, 1989), p. 175. Another statement by Gandhi about Thoreau is in Webb Miller, *I Found No Peace* (Garden City, N.Y.: Garden City Publishing Co., 1938), pp. 238–239.

Gandhi's introduction and extracts from "Civil Disobedience," in Gujarati, were published in *Indian Opinion*, September 7, 1907. The English translation appears in *Collected Works of Mahatma Gandhi*, VII:217–218. The second collection of extracts, in Gujarati but translated into English, is in VII:228–230. The two articles in Gujarati were then published as a pamphlet priced 6d, postage 7d. Gandhi's introduction about Thoreau and extracts from "Civil Disobedience," both in English, appeared in *Indian Opinion*, October 26, 1907, and were reprinted in *Collected Works of Mahatma Gandhi*, VII:304–305.

The article about Socrates appeared in *Indian Opinion*, November 16, 1907, p. 475. Gandhi's article on Socrates, in Gujarati, was later banned in India, as was his edition of Ruskin's *Unto This Last: A Paraphrase*.

The account of Gandhi's reading during his first imprisonment is from his *Speeches and Writings* (Madras: Natesan, 1933), p. 218.

Gandhi describes the first settlement with Smuts in 1908 in *Satyagraha in South Africa*, pp. 239–243. The controversy about the settlement and the physical attack on Gandhi are from pp. 244–267. The comparison to the Boston Tea Party is from p. 314.

Gandhi's reading during his second stay in jail is from his *Speeches and Writings*, p. 226–228.

Payne in *Life and Death of Mahatma Gandhi* has a useful description of Gandhi's third stay in jail, pp. 193–195. Payne gives a clear account of Gandhi's trip to London in 1909, pp. 199–219.

We have used the Gandhi-Tolstoy correspondence published in Kalidas Nag, *Tolstoy and Gandhi* (Patna: Pustak Bhandar, 1950). The quote from Tolstoy's first letter to Gandhi is on p. 63.

Payne publishes Gandhi's "Confession of Faith, 1909" in *Life and Death of Mahatma Gandhi*, pp. 215–217.

We used Gandhi's extensive account of Tolstoy Farm in *Satyagraha in South Africa*, pp. 354–393. The account of the strike and the march into Transvaal is from pp. 434–463. The end of the struggle is from pp. 498–508.

Payne in *Life and Death of Mahatma Gandhi*, pp. 330–331, is particularly good on the Rowlatt Act. For an account of the massacre at Amritsar, see pp. 337–345. The quote about the bloodletting at Amritsar is from p. 339. Payne gives a good account of Gandhi's career in India after returning from South Africa. The extended accounts by Pyarelal and Tendulkar should be consulted for more detailed information.

Chapter VII: The Walls of Segregation Go Up Once More

The quotation from "Go Down, Moses" is from Hill, *Call and Response*, p. 44.

For general information in this chapter we have used Franklin and Moss, *From Slavery to Freedom*. For the number of black voters in Louisiana and DuBois's quote on blacks being moved back toward slavery, see p. 288.

Additional background information is from Hine, Hine, and Harrold, *African-American Odyssey*. The quote about the black women who was lynched is from pp. 319–320. The information about segregation on Southern streetcars is from p. 315. On blacks in World War I, see pp. 376–378. For information about DuBois and Booker T. Washington, pp. 361–370.

For information about DuBois's publishing articles on Gandhi's civil disobedience, see Sudarshan Kapur, *Raising Up a Prophet: The African-American Encounter with Gandhi* (Boston: Beacon Press, 1992), pp. 24–28. For Frazier's doubts about the Gandhian method, pp. 34–36.

For information on the rebirth of the Klan, see Wade, *Fiery Cross*, pp. 119–166.

For background information about Marcus Garvey, see Hine, Hine, and Harrold, *African-American Odyssey*, pp. 399–402. For the quote about Garvey's appeal, see *From Slavery to Freedom*, p. 396.

For information about Dr. Benjamin E. Mays, see Stephen B. Oates, *Let the Trumpet Sound: The Life of Martin Luther King, Jr.* (New York: Harper & Row, 1982), pp. 19–20, and the Mays entry in *American National Biography*, 14:795–796. Kapur, *Raising Up a Prophet*, was used for quotations about Mays's interview with Gandhi, p. 94; Gandhi on working with a minority, p. 95; and on what blacks can learn from Indians, p. 37.

Kapur, *Raising Up a Prophet*, was also used for "Wanted: A Black Reformer," p. 50. On Gandhi as a Christ figure, see p. 55. On blacks urged not to pay taxes, see p. 57. On Richard Gregg's handbook on nonviolence and his letter to DuBois, see p. 47.

For information about A. Philip Randolph, see Hine, Hine, and Harrold, *African-American Odyssey*, pp. 404–405; *American National Biography*, 18:117–120.

For information about blacks at the University of Illinois before World War II, we used the *Daily Illini*, February 20, 2004, p. A-8.

For Randolph's December 1940 beginning plan for a march on Washington, see Kapur, *Raising Up a Prophet*, p. 102. On a mass movement campaign, p. 102.

For additional information on Randolph and the March on Washington movement, see Hine, Hine, and Harrold, *African-American Odyssey*, pp. 473–475. The quote from Executive Order #8802 is from p. 475.

On Randolph's differences from Gandhism, see Kapur, *Raising Up a Prophet*, pp. 113–114.

For background information on Bayard Rustin we have used John D'Emilio's *Lost Prophet: The Life and Times of Bayard Rustin* (New York: Free Press, 2003). For Rustin on nonviolence as a way of life, see p. 54. On the difficulty of presenting nonviolence to Negro people, p. 55.

Deb Aronson wrote the article about black students at the University of Illinois at Urbana-Champaign after World War II:

"'Against All Odds' FBIs Succeed Despite Racism on Campus," *Illinois Alumni*, January/February 2002, pp. 54–55 (FBI stands for Fifties Black Illini).

For an account of the Legal Defense and Educational Fund of the NAACP, see Hine, Hine, and Harrold, *African-American Odyssey*, pp. 489–490.

The text of *Brown v. Board of Education* is contained in Franklin and Moss, *From Slavery to Freedom*. The quote from that text is from p. 691.

For the importance of the *Brown* ruling, see Hine, Hine, and Harrold, *African-American Odyssey*, p. 493. There are many books and articles on *Brown*; we have found useful James T. Patterson, *Brown v. Board of Education: A Civil Rights Milestone and Its Troubled Legacy* (New York: Oxford University Press, 2002).

The defiant quotation from the Mississippi judge is quoted in Bennett, *Before the Mayflower*, p. 348.

The section on Emmett Till is indebted to Hine, Hine, and Harrold, *African-American Odyssey*, p. 503.

Chapter VIII. "Trumpets Begin to Sound": Martin Luther King, Jr., and the Beginnings of the Civil Disobedience Movement

The quotation from "Joshua Fit de Battle of Jericho" is from Hill, *Call and Response*, p. 47.

For biographical information about Rosa Parks, we have used Douglas Brinkley, *Rosa Parks* (New York: Viking, 2000). Her confrontation with the bus driver is from pp. 106–107.

Parks on why she did not move from her seat is from her *Quiet Strength* (Grand Rapids, Mich.: Zondervan, 1994), p. 22.

Brinkley in *Rosa Parks* describes her early life, pp. 11–27.

Parks's quotation about her grandfather protecting his house is from *Quiet Strength*, p. 16; her quote about defending herself is from pp. 16–17.

Brinkley in *Rosa Parks* discusses Parks's work for E. D. Nixon, pp. 50–56. Information about the Durr family and Parks's relationship with them, pp. 78–86. Parks and the Highlander Folk

School, pp. 91–97. Parks's arrest, booking, release, and the discussion about a test case, pp. 98–118.

For E. D. Nixon's efforts to organize a boycott, see David J. Garrow, *Bearing the Cross: Martin Luther King, Jr., and the Southern Christian Leadership Conference* (New York: William Morrow, 1986), pp. 12–19. The text of the leaflet announcing the boycott is on pp. 16–17.

The list of King's extensive church duties is from *The Papers of Martin Luther King, Jr.* (Berkeley: University of California Press, 1994), II:581.

Information about the activities and meetings before the Monday boycott are from Garrow, *Bearing the Cross*, pp. 17–22.

The account of the Monday afternoon meeting is from Taylor Branch, *Parting the Waters: America in the King Years, 1954–63* (New York: Simon and Schuster, 1988), pp. 136–137. Speculation on why the established preachers deferred to King is from p. 137.

King's December 5, 1955, speech and the Abernathy proposals are from *Papers of Martin Luther King, Jr.*, III:71–79. The paraphrase of the text of the telegram to the management of the Montgomery bus lines (headquartered in Chicago), containing three proposals, is from III:80–81.

For biographical information about King we have used the introductions, texts, and notes in *Papers of Martin Luther King, Jr.*, vols. I–IV. We have also used Branch's *Parting the Waters*; Garrow's *Bearing the Cross*; Oates's *Let the Trumpet Sound*; Peter J. Ling, *Martin Luther King, Jr.* (London: Routledge, 2002); David L. Lewis, *King: A Biography* (Urbana: University of Illinois Press, 1978); Clayborne Carson, ed., *The Autobiography of Martin Luther King, Jr.* (New York: Warner Books, 2001); and Michael Eric Dyson, *I May Not Get There with You: The True Martin Luther King, Jr.* (New York: Simon and Schuster, 2000).

The introductions to *The Papers of Martin Luther King, Jr.* and Oates, *Let the Trumpet Sound*, provide useful information about Reverend Williams and Reverend King, Sr., and their families.

Lewis, in *King*, discusses King's professors at Morehouse, pp. 18–21. The biographical notes in *Papers of Martin Luther King, Jr.* are particularly helpful for the Morehouse years.

King's reaction to Thoreau's "Civil Disobedience" is from his *Stride Toward Freedom* (New York: Harper, 1958), p. 91. King wrote George Hendrick, February 5, 1957, that he had read most of the major works of Gandhi and Thoreau's "Civil Disobedience" before he arrived in Montgomery and that both had deeply influenced his thinking. Quotations from that letter, now in the Rare Book and Special Collections Library, University of Illinois at Urbana-Champaign, are in *Papers of Martin Luther King, Jr.*, IV:184n.

King's Morehouse transcript, with grades, is from *Papers of Martin Luther King, Jr.*, I:39–40. His Crozer transcript, with grades, is from I:48.

Professor Williams on King at Morehouse is from Lewis, *King*, p. 20.

For King on his private philosophical studies while a student at Crozer, see his *Stride Toward Freedom*, pp. 91–93.

For information on Muste and Mordecai Johnson, see Kapur, *Raising Up a Prophet*, pp. 85–86, 120. Both men have biographical sketches in *American National Biography*. King wrote about hearing Muste and Johnson speak in *Stride Toward Freedom*, pp. 95–97.

The summary of Johnson's speech about Gandhi is from Kapur, *Raising Up a Prophet*, pp. 146–147.

The quote from Fischer's *Life of Mahatma Gandhi* is on p. 275. King on Gandhi is from *Stride Toward Freedom*, p. 97.

Stephen Oates, in *Let the Trumpet Sound*, quotes Juliette Morgan's letter to the editor about Thoreau and Gandhi, pp. 73–74. See also *Papers of Martin Luther King, Jr.*, III:17, 36, 85n5.

For an extended account of King's first arrest, see *Stride Toward Freedom*, pp. 127–131. He describes the bombing of his house on pp. 135–140.

The quote by the frightened policeman at the bombed home of the Kings is from Oates, *Let the Trumpet Sound*, pp. 86–87.

Background information on Bayard Rustin is from D'Emilio, *Lost Prophet*. Rustin's meeting with Abernathy and Nixon, p. 228. His comments on King's coming to an understanding of Gandhi, pp. 230–231.

King on love as "redemptive good will" is from *Stride Toward Freedom*, p. 104.

The quotations from Jo Ann Robinson about her problems with the police are from Henry Hampton and Steve Fayer, *Voices of Freedom: An Oral History of the Civil Rights Movement from the 1950s Through the 1980s* (New York: Bantam Books, 1990), p. 31.

Chapter IX. A Better Day

The lines from "There's a Better Day a Coming" are from Hill, *Call and Response*, p. 236.

Information about Jasper, Tex., and the murder of James Byrd, Jr., is from Pamela Colloff, "Jasper: What Happens to a Town Identified with One of the Worst Hate Crimes in American History?" in *Texas Monthly*, December 2003, pp. 154–159, 176–184. All direct quotes are from this article.

Michael Eric Dyson, in *I May Not Get There with You*, in Chapter 12, "The Ownership of a Great Man," writes perceptively about the activities of the King Estate, the fight with Boston University over his papers, problems with the library and museum in Atlanta, and much else. Dyson is also particularly good in his discussions of King's plagiarism and his infidelities.

The Socrates quotation is from *The Apology of Socrates* reprinted in Crawford, *Civil Disobedience*, p. 11. The Gandhi quotation is from the same book, p. 212.

The Thoreau quotation from "Civil Disobedience" is from the last paragraph of that essay.

We wish to thank Ivan R. Dee for his advice and careful editing of our manuscript. We are also indebted to Hilary Meyer for her help in finding illustrations for this book.

INDEX

A NOTE ON THE AUTHORS

George Hendrick and Willene Hendrick, independent scholars, together have written *The Creole Mutiny: A Tale of Revolt Aboard a Slave Ship* and have edited *Incidents in the Life of a Slave Girl and A True Tale of Slavery*; *Two Slave Rebellions at Sea*; and *Fleeing for Freedom: Stories of the Undergound Railroad as Told by Levi Coffin and William Still*. They have also published *Selected Poems of Carl Sandburg*; Sandburg's *Poems for the People* and *Billy Sunday and Other Poems*; and books on Katherine Anne Porter, Hiram Rutherford, Henry Salt, and Ham Jones. They live in Urbana, Illinois.